LEARN
Adobe Illustrator CC
for Graphic Design and Illustration

Adobe Certified Associate Exam Preparation

Dena Wilson
and Peter Lourekas
with Rob Schwartz

ADOBE
PRESS

Adobe

LEARN ADOBE ILLUSTRATOR CC FOR GRAPHIC DESIGN AND ILLUSTRATION
ADOBE CERTIFIED ASSOCIATE EXAM PREPARATION
Dena Wilson and **Peter Lourekas**
with **Rob Schwartz**

Copyright © 2016 by Peachpit Press

Adobe Press books are published by Peachpit, a division of Pearson Education.
For the latest on Adobe Press books and videos, go to www.adobepress.com.
To report errors, please send a note to errata@peachpit.com

Adobe Press Editor: Victor Gavenda
Senior Editor, Video: Karyn Johnson
Development Editors (book and video): Bob Lindstrom, Stephen Nathans-Kelly
Technical Reviewer: Chad Chelius
Copyeditor: Kelly Anton
Senior Production Editors: Becky Winter, Tracey Croom
Compositor: Kim Scott, Bumpy Design
Proofreader: Liz Welch
Indexer: Rebecca Plunkett
Cover & Interior Design: Mimi Heft
Cover Illustration: Sylverarts, Fotolia.com

ISBN-13: 978-0-13-439778-8
ISBN-10: 0-13-439778-9

2   17
Printed and bound in the United States of America

Acknowledgments

I would like to thank the following people for their contributions to this project:

Rob Schwartz, a friend and colleague for life! Thank you for having enough faith in me to get me involved!

Peter Lourekas, who has been invaluable as a resource, sounding board, and encourager extraordinaire! Thank you!

My past and present graphics students who asked me to teach them "everything" and made me push myself even harder!

And also to Victor Gavenda, Stephen Nathans-Kelly, and the editing crew who kept me on track and running smoothly! Many thanks!

—Dena Wilson

My sincere thanks go to all the members of the Editorial and Production teams who helped to turn my words into a book: Victor Gavenda, Adobe Press Editor; Bob Lindstrom and Stephen Nathans-Kelly, development editors; Chad Chelius, technical reviewer; Kelly Anton, copyeditor; Liz Welch, proofreader; Tracey Croom, Senior Production Editor; Kim Scott of Bumpy Design, compositor; and Mimi Heft, cover and interior design.

Thanks also to Matt Niemitz and Remy Mansfield of Adobe Education Programs for help with this project.

I would like to include a special thank-you to my co-author Dena Wilson for producing artful and inspiring visual projects—along with their accompanying graphics—that made the writing assignment fun and enjoyable.

—Peter Lourekas

About the Authors

Dena Wilson (video author) is a graphic artist and dedicated educator. She is an avid Adobe Illustrator user and has taught graphic design for over 12 years at both the high school and collegiate level.

Dena's expertise is in the delivery of hands-on, skill-based instruction both online and in the classroom. Her high school students enjoy a passing rate above 80 percent on the Adobe ACA certification exam. She was on the original team of writers for the ACA exam for Adobe Photoshop and served as an Adobe Education Leader for many years. Dena is an Adobe Certified Associate in Illustrator and Photoshop.

As an expert author, **Peter Lourekas** (primary book author) knows the power of visual learning. For two decades, he has been a co-author (with Elaine Weinmann) of the best-selling Visual QuickStart guides to Photoshop and Illustrator—the top choice in college classrooms and the go-to reference for design professionals. These guides have sold more than 3.5 million copies worldwide.

Peter has co-authored the Photoshop and Illustrator courseware for the MyGraphicsLab digital learning product series published by Pearson Education and has taught at Cooper Union School of Art, the New School, and Parsons School of Design.

Rob Schwartz (author of book chapters 18 and 19) is an award-winning teacher (currently at Sheridan Technical College in Hollywood, FL) with over 15 years' experience in technical education. Rob holds several Adobe Certified Associate certifications, and is also an Adobe Certified Instructor. As an Adobe Education Leader Rob won the prestigious Impact Award from Adobe, and in 2010 Rob was the first winner of the Certiport Adobe Certified Associate World Championship. Find out more about Rob at his online curriculum website at brainbuffet.com.

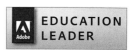

Contents

To access your free copy of this book's Web Edition containing more than 6 hours of video, see the instructions on pp. xi–xii.

Getting Started

Welcome to *Learn Adobe Illustrator CC for Graphic Design and Illustration!* This product uses a combination of text and video to help you learn the basics of graphic design and illustration with Adobe Illustrator CC along with other skills that you will need to get your first job as a graphic designer or illustrator. Adobe Illustrator CC is a powerful program for creating illustrations, logos, icons, and graphic designs composed of type and vector art that can be scaled, transformed, recolored, and reshaped at any time without any loss of quality. Various editable effects can be applied to shapes or type to further stylize the objects in your artwork. You can also use Illustrator to output your artwork as printed pieces or to export the artwork to video and web applications for viewing on screen and mobile devices.

About This Product

Learn Adobe Illustrator CC for Graphic Design and Illustration was created by a team of expert instructors, writers, and editors with years of experience in helping beginning learners get their start with the cool creative tools from Adobe. Our aim is not only to teach you the basics of the art of graphic design and illustration with Illustrator, but to give you an introduction to the associated "soft" skills (like design principles and project management) that you'll need for your first job.

We've built the training around the objectives for the Graphic Design and Illustration Using Adobe Illustrator CC Adobe Certified Associate Exam, and if you master the topics covered in this book and video you'll be in good shape to take the exam. But even if certification isn't your goal, you'll still find this training will give you an excellent foundation for your future work in graphic design and illustration.

This product is a unique learning system that uses video and text in partnership. You'll experience this partnership in action in the Web Edition, which lives on your Account page at peachpit.com. The Web Edition contains 6 hours of video—the heart of the training—embedded in an online eBook that supports the video training and provides background material. The eBook material is also sold separately for offline reading as a printed book or an eBook in a variety of formats. The Web Edition also includes dozens of interactive review questions you can use to evaluate your progress, as well as a chapter on principles of design (Chapter 19). Purchase of the book in *any* format entitles you to free access to the Web Edition (instructions for accessing it follow later in this section).

Most chapters provide step-by-step instructions for creating a specific project or learning a specific technique. Other chapters acquaint you with other skills and concepts that you'll come to depend on as you use the software in the workaday world. You can follow the book from start to finish or work through only the chapters that meet your interests and needs. Many chapters include several optional tasks that let you further explore the features you've already learned.

Each chapter opens with two lists of objectives. One list lays out the learning objectives: the specific tasks you'll learn in the chapter. The second list shows the ACA exam objectives that are covered in the chapter. A table at the end of the book guides you to coverage of all of the exam objectives in the book or video.

Conventions Used in This Book

This book uses several elements styled in ways to help you as you work through the projects.

Text that you should enter appears in bold, such as:

> In the Link field in the Property inspector, type **https://helpx.adobe.com/illustrator/topics.html**.

Terms that are defined in the Glossary appear in bold and in color, such as:

> In Illustrator CC, you use the drawing tools on the Tools panel to create **shapes**.

Links to videos that cover the topics in depth appear in the margins.

The ACA objectives covered in the chapters are called out in the margins beside the sections that address them.

▶ *Video Project*
01-01 Basic Shape—Live Shapes

★ *ACA Objective 2.1*

Notes and Tips give additional information about a topic. The information they contain is not essential to accomplishing a task but provides a more in-depth understanding of the topic.

> **NOTE** *If your line segment has a stroke of white color, or a small stroke weight, it may be hard to see. See "Working with Fill and Stroke" in this chapter to learn how to edit the color.*

> **TIP** *To create a line segment by entering values, click the Line Segment tool where you want the line to begin. In the dialog box, enter a Length value and an Angle value, and click OK.*

OPERATING SYSTEM DIFFERENCES

In most cases, Illustrator CC works the same in both Windows and Mac OS X. Minor differences exist between the two versions, mostly due to platform-specific issues. Most of these are simply differences in keyboard shortcuts, how dialog boxes are displayed, and how buttons are named. In most cases, screen shots were made in the Mac OS version of Ilustrator CC and may appear somewhat differently from your own screen.

Where specific commands differ, they are noted within the text. Mac OS commands are listed first, followed by the Windows equivalent, such as Command+C/Ctrl+C In general, the Windows Ctrl key is equivalent to the Command (or "Cmd") key in Mac OS and the Windows Alt key is equivalent to the Option (or "Opt") key in Mac OS.

As lessons proceed, instructions may be truncated or shortened to save space, with the assumption that you picked up the essential concepts earlier in the lesson. For example, at the beginning of a lesson you may be instructed to "press Cmd+C/Ctrl+C." Later, you may be told to "copy" text or a code element. These should be considered identical instructions.

If you find you have difficulties in any particular task, review earlier steps or exercises in that lesson. In some cases if an exercise is based on concepts covered earlier, you will be referred back to the specific lesson.

Installing the Software

Before you begin using *Learn Adobe Illustrator CC for Graphic Design and Illustration*, make sure that your system is set up correctly and that you've installed the proper software and hardware. This material is based on the July 2015 release of Adobe Illustrator CC 2015 (version 19.1.0) and is designed to cover the objectives of the Adobe Certified Associate Exam for that version of the software.

The Adobe Illustrator CC software is not included with this book; it is available only with an Adobe Creative Cloud membership. You must purchase a membership or it must be supplied by your school or other organization. In addition to Adobe Illustrator CC, some lessons in this book have steps that can be performed with Adobe Photoshop. You must install these applications from Adobe Creative Cloud onto your computer. Follow the instructions provided at *helpx.adobe.com/creative-cloud/help/download-install-app.html*.

CHECKING FOR UPDATES

Adobe periodically provides updates to software. You can easily obtain these updates through the Creative Cloud. If these updates include new features that affect the content of this training or the objectives of the ACA exam in any way, we will post updated material to peachpit.com.

Accessing the Free Web Edition and Lesson Files

Your purchase of this product in any format includes access to the corresponding Web Edition hosted on peachpit.com. The Web Edition contains the complete text of the book (including an additional bonus chapter) augmented with hours of video and interactive quizzes.

To work through the projects in this product, you will first need to download the lesson files from peachpit.com. You can download the files for individual lessons or download them all in a single file.

If you purchased an eBook from peachpit.com or adobepress.com, the Web Edition will automatically appear under the Digital Purchases tab on your Account page. Click the Launch link to access the product. Continue reading to learn how to register your product to get access to the lesson files.

If you purchased an eBook from a different vendor or you bought a print book, you must register your purchase on peachpit.com:

1 Go to *www.peachpit.com/register*.

2 Sign in or create a new account.

3 Enter ISBN: **9780134397788**.

4 Answer the questions as proof of purchase.

5 The **Web Edition** will appear under the Digital Purchases tab on your Account page. Click the Launch link to access the product.

   The **Lesson Files** can be accessed through the Registered Products tab on your Account page. Click the Access Bonus Content link below the title of your product to proceed to the download page. Click the lesson file links to download them to your computer.

Additional Resources

Learn Adobe Illustrator CC for Graphic Design and Illustration is not meant to replace documentation that comes with the program or to be a comprehensive reference for every feature. For comprehensive information about program features and tutorials, refer to these resources:

Adobe Illustrator Learn & Support: *helpx.adobe.com/illustrator/topics.html* is where you can find and browse Help and Support content on Adobe.com. Adobe Illustrator Help and Adobe Illustrator Support Center are accessible from the Help menu in Illustrator. Help is also available as a printable PDF document. Download the document at *helpx.adobe.com/pdf/illustrator_reference.pdf*.

Adobe Forums: *forums.adobe.com* lets you tap into peer-to-peer discussions, questions, and answers on Adobe products.

Adobe Illustrator product home page: *adobe.com/products/illustrator* provides information about new features and intuitive ways to create professional layouts for print, tablets, and eBooks.

Adobe Add-ons: *creative.adobe.com/addons* is a central resource for finding tools, services, extensions, code samples, and more to supplement and extend your Adobe products.

Resources for educators: *adobe.com/education* and *edex.adobe.com* offer a treasure trove of information for instructors who teach classes on Adobe software. Find solutions for education at all levels, including free curricula that use an integrated approach to teaching Adobe software and can be used to prepare for the Adobe Certified Associate exams.

Adobe Certification

The Adobe training and certification programs are designed to help Adobe customers improve and promote their product-proficiency skills. The Adobe Certified Associate (ACA) is an industry-recognized credential that demonstrates proficiency in Adobe digital skills. Whether you're just starting out in your career, looking to switch jobs, or interested in preparing students for success in the job market, the Adobe Certified Associate program is for you! For more information visit *edex.adobe.com/aca*.

Resetting the Preferences to Their Default Settings

Adobe Illustrator CC lets you determine how the program looks and behaves using the extensive options in Illustrator CC > Preferences (Mac OS) or Edit > Preferences (Windows). These settings for parameters such as tool settings and the default unit of measurement are stored in a file called Adobe Illustrator Prefs (Mac OS) or AIPrefs (Windows). To ensure that the preferences and default settings of your Adobe Illustrator program match those used in this book, you can reset your preference settings to their defaults. If you're using software installed on computers in a classroom, don't make any changes to the system configuration without first checking with your instructor.

To reset your preferences to their default settings, follow these steps:

1 Quit Adobe Illustrator CC.

2 Hold down the Cmd+Opt+Shift keys (Mac OS) or Ctrl+Alt+Shift keys (Windows).

3 Continue to hold the keys and start Adobe Illustrator CC.

4 When the program's splash screen appears, release the keys. Your preferences will be deleted and the program's default settings will be restored.

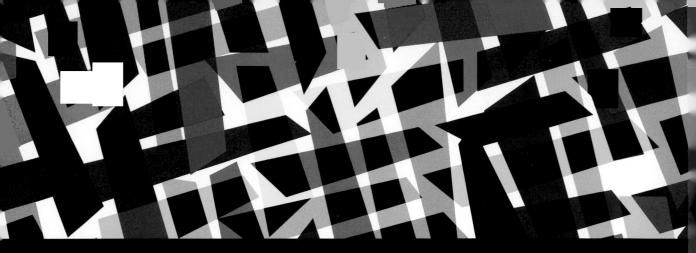

CHAPTER OBJECTIVES

Chapter Learning Objectives

- Explore the Illustrator interface.
- Use the main interface elements.
- Explore the essential panels.
- Create and modify workspaces

Chapter ACA Objectives

DOMAIN 3.0
UNDERSTANDING ADOBE ILLUSTRATOR CC

3.1 Identify elements of the Illustrator user interface and demonstrate knowledge of their functions.

3.3 Navigate, organize, and customize the workspace.

CHAPTER 1

Introduction to Adobe Illustrator CC

Adobe Illustrator CC is the premier vector drawing application. A vector application creates shapes composed of points, lines, and curves that are stored as mathematical instructions as opposed to a bitmap application, which creates shapes composed of pixel dots. A wide array of print and screen designers use Illustrator to create designs and artwork. In combination with the instructional videos, this book will help you master the various tools and commands found in Illustrator CC.

Illustrator CC Interface

The Illustrator CC interface contains the tools, panels, menu commands, document window, and artboards you will use when creating or editing an Illustrator document. The interface can be customized to fit your work style. You can selectively open and group panels based on your design needs, expand or collapse displayed panels, open two or more documents, and save any custom interface configurations for repeated use.

Before you get to the hands-on tasks for creating an Illustrator document, you'll find it helpful to examine the key parts of the Illustrator CC interface. So launch Illustrator CC and open the supplied document Shapes1.ai in the Intro-01 Workarea folder.

NOTE

This chapter supports the Video Intro. Go to the Video Intro page in the book's Web Edition to watch the entire video intro from beginning to end.

Application Frame

The entire Illustrator interface is housed within the **Application frame** (**Figure 1.1**).

- **Windows:** In Windows, the Application frame is always visible—it's just another term for the application window. To minimize the Application frame in Windows, click the Minimize button.

- **Mac OS:** In Mac OS, the Application frame is displayed by default. We highly recommend that Mac users keep the frame visible for two reasons: first, to block out the distraction of a cluttered desktop, and second, to organize all open document windows and panels within a movable and resizable frame. To show the Application frame, choose Window > Application Frame. A check mark will appear next to the command and the frame will appear onscreen. To minimize the frame in Mac OS, click the yellow Minimize button.

TIP

Drag any edge or corner of the frame to resize it. Drag the top bar of the frame to reposition the entire frame.

Figure 1.1 The Application frame

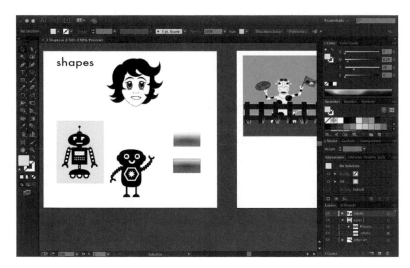

★ *ACA Objective 3.1*

▶ *Video Intro 01*
Work Area

Using the Main Interface Elements

The main interface elements in Illustrator CC that you will examine are as follows:

- The Application bar
- The Control panel
- The Tools panel
- Panels (to the right of the Application frame)
- Workspaces

Application Bar

Click the buttons on the **Application bar** (**Figure 1.2**) to quickly switch to the **Adobe Bridge** application or to access the Adobe Stock website. Choose options from the **Arrange Documents menu** to arrange multiple document windows within the Application frame. From the **workspace switcher menu** you can access and manage workspaces. Enter a keyword or phrase in the Search For Help field, and then press Return/Enter to display information on your query in your default browser.

Go to Bridge · Current workspace · Search for Help field · Arrange Documents menu · Workspace switcher menu

Figure 1.2 Controls accessible from the Application bar (in Mac OS)

Control Panel

Frequently used controls and settings appear on the **Control panel** (**Figure 1.3**) for easy access. The panel options change depending on the tool or type of object currently selected (**Figure 1.4**). You can use this panel to apply fill and stroke colors; change an object's variable width profile, brush stroke definition, or opacity; apply basic type attributes; align and distribute multiple objects; and access controls for editing symbols, Image Trace, Live Paint objects, and placed images.

You can also quickly access the Document Setup or **Preferences** dialog box by clicking the button with that respective name.

> **TIP** Click the various underlined option name links (such as Transform; the X, Y, W, or H fields; Opacity; or Stroke) or click the arrow next to any menu (such as the Fill or Stroke square menu, Style menu, or Brush Definition menu) to open a temporary version of the panel that manages each function.

Figure 1.3 Options available on the Control panel when an object is selected with the Selection tool

Figure 1.4 Options available on the Control panel when an anchor point is selected with the Direct Selection tool

Figure 1.5 The Tools panel with a menu of shape tools displayed

TIP

To toggle the Tools panel between a single-column and two-column layout, click the double arrowhead at the top of the panel.

TIP

To show or hide the Tools panel, choose Window > Tools > Default. A check mark will appear in the menu when the panel is visible.

NOTE

Some tools (such as the Paintbrush, Blob Brush, Pencil, Shape Builder, and Blend tools) display an options dialog box when you double-click its icon or select the tool and press Return/Enter.

Tools Panel

The **Tools panel**, also called the toolbar, contains tools used for selecting, drawing, and editing objects (**Figure 1.5**). It also includes controls for choosing color, a menu for choosing one of three **drawing modes**, and a menu for choosing one of three screen modes.

Related tools are grouped together on the panel. Click a visible tool icon to select it. Hold down the mouse button on a tool that displays a tiny arrow to choose from hidden tools. Option-click (Mac OS) or Alt-click (Windows) a tool icon to cycle through all the tools within its related group.

To quickly choose a tool, press the letter shortcut that is assigned to it. Keyboard shortcuts are listed in the tool tips that display when you place the pointer over a tool icon and in tool menus.

Create a Tearoff Toolbar

You can create a free-floating mini-toolbar that contains only the tools that display on a hidden toolbar menu.

To create a tearoff toolbar:

1　Hold down the mouse button on a tool icon to display its hidden tools.

2　Click the vertical bar on the right edge of the hidden tools menu.

3　Drag the dark gray bar at the top of the toolbar to tear off the menu and reposition it.

4　Double-click the dark gray bar to switch the tearoff toolbar to a vertical orientation.

5　Click the tearoff toolbar's close button to close it.

Create Custom Tools Panels

For a more efficient drawing and editing workflow, you can create custom tools panels that contain only tools you use for specific tasks. For example, you might create one panel that contains drawing tools and another that contains reshaping tools. Once created, a custom tools panel can be opened from the Window > Tools submenu.

To create a free-floating custom tools panel:

1 Choose Window > Tools > New Tools Panel.

2 In the New Tools panel dialog box, enter a name for the new tools panel.

3 Click OK.

A new, blank panel displays in the Application frame (**Figure 1.6**), containing Fill and Stroke buttons.

4 Drag a tool from the default Tools panel into the upper area of the custom panel (**Figure 1.7**). When the pointer becomes an arrowhead with a **plus (+)** symbol, release the mouse button. The tool icon will appear on the custom panel (**Figure 1.8**).

Figure 1.6 A blank custom tools panel

Figure 1.7 Drag to add a tool to the new custom tools panel.

Figure 1.8 The new tool displays on the panel.

5 Repeat this method to add additional tools to the custom panel.

6 To remove a tool from the custom panel, drag it out of the panel.

7 To reposition a tool within a custom panel, drag it to the desired location, and release the mouse button when the horizontal drop zone bar appears.

TIP

Use the Manage Tools Panel dialog box (Window > Tools) to rename, duplicate, or delete a custom tools panel.

Panels

Panels are an indispensable part of the Illustrator interface. They contain options and settings that enable you to quickly modify the **attributes** of one or more selected objects in your artwork.

Panels provide additional options in panel menus, which you display by clicking the panel menu icon ( ). You can quickly display or open panels to access their options, then minimize or close them to save space onscreen. Pretty cool!

By default, the Illustrator interface docks together several groups of panels at the right of the Application frame.

You have already learned about the Control panel and Tools panel, but Illustrator includes more than 35 panels. Learn to work with the essential ones first. For your initial encounter with panels, start by exploring the following key panels:

- Color
- Swatches
- Stroke
- Appearance
- Transform

Color Panel

In Illustrator, you can apply color to an object's fill (interior) or stroke (edge). In the Color panel (**Figure 1.9**), the first thing you will do is click the Fill or Stroke square so Illustrator knows what to do. In fact, when applying color to selected objects, selecting the Fill or Stroke square is such an essential first step that these indicators are located on the Color, Swatches, Control, Appearance, Gradient, and Tools panels. Clicking the Fill or Stroke square on one of these six panels automatically makes it active on the other panels.

To use the Color panel:

1 Select an object to which you want to apply color.

2 Specify whether you want to fill or stroke an object by clicking either the Fill or the Stroke square.

3 Drag the color sliders or click in the spectrum bar at the bottom of the panel to apply a color to the selected Fill/Stroke square and to any selected objects in your document.

4 Click the panel menu icon to display its menu and choose a color model for the panel, such as RGB or CMYK.

TIP

Expand the spectrum bar by dragging down the lower edge of the panel.

Figure 1.9 The Color panel

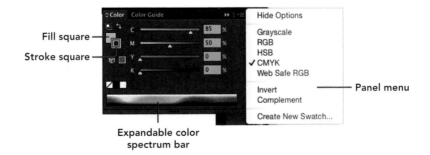

Fill square

Stroke square

Panel menu

Expandable color spectrum bar

Swatches Panel

Use the Swatches panel (**Figure 1.10**) to store and apply solid colors, **patterns**, and **gradients** to objects in your Illustrator document. On the panel, click either the Fill or the Stroke square, and then click a swatch to apply the color to one or more selected objects. Drag a copy of either square onto the blank area of the Swatches panel (or click the New Swatch button at the bottom of the panel) to save a color, pattern, or gradient to the panel.

TIP *Many panel menus provide options for customizing the panel; for example, the Swatches panel offers an option for thumbnail display size.*

Stroke Panel

Options and settings found on the Stroke panel (**Figure 1.11**) control the appearance of an object's path (edge). Use this panel to specify a **stroke weight** (thickness), a cap (end of a path) style, and a corner style for a path, and to choose how a stroke is aligned (positioned) on a path. The panel also provides options for creating dashed lines, applying an arrowhead and/or tail to a path, and applying a **variable-width profile** to a path.

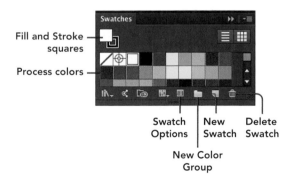

Fill and Stroke squares

Process colors

Swatch Options

New Swatch

Delete Swatch

New Color Group

Figure 1.10 The Swatches panel

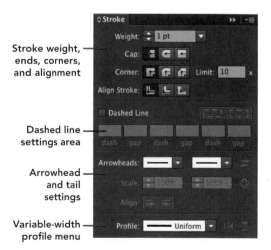

Stroke weight, ends, corners, and alignment

Dashed line settings area

Arrowhead and tail settings

Variable-width profile menu

Figure 1.11 The Stroke panel

Appearance Panel

An object in Illustrator can have specific appearance attributes applied to it (such as fill and stroke color, stroke width, opacity, and effects). The Appearance panel (**Figure 1.12**) lists the attributes and settings for the currently selected object, group, or layer. In this panel, you can add, modify, or remove object, group, or layer attributes.

Convenient in-panel features (similar to the linked features found in the Control panel) enable you to quickly access temporary panels and dialog boxes to edit settings. For example, click the underlined word "Stroke" to open a temporary Stroke panel or click a color square (or its arrow) to open a temporary Swatches panel.

As you work more with Illustrator, you will find the Appearance panel to be a central part of your editing workflow.

Transform Panel

The upper portion of the Transform panel (**Figure 1.13**) lists values for the X and Y coordinates, width, height, rotation angle, and shear angle of a selected object. You can edit the value in a field to modify that object setting.

The middle portion of the panel displays the shape properties (width, height, and corner settings) for any selected object drawn with the Rectangle or Rounded Rectangle tool.

The lower area of the panel provides options that you can turn on or off to control specific attributes related to scaling an object.

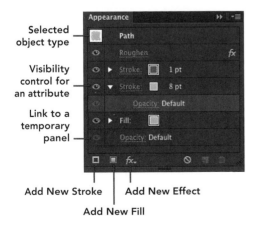

Figure 1.12 The Appearance panel

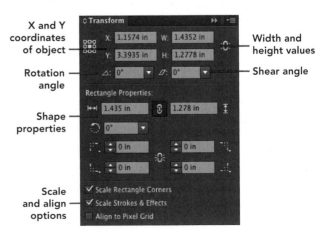

Figure 1.13 The Transform panel

Workspaces

★ *ACA Objective 3.3*

Workspaces are custom arrangements of the panels and panel groups in the **dock**, along with any user-created tools panels, floating tearoff toolbars, and custom tools panels.

▶ *Video Intro 03*
Workspaces

To help you immediately get started with custom workspaces and their potential, Illustrator has provided eight predefined workspaces: Essentials (composed of 13 key panels) along with Automation, Layout, Painting, Printing and Proofing, Tracing, Typography, and Web (created for specific design workflows).

On the Control panel, use the workspace switcher menu to switch between these eight predefined workspaces. As you display each workspace, take note of which panels Adobe selected to support a specific design workflow.

Create a Custom Workspace

Rather than repeatedly reconfigure the panels at the beginning of each work session, you can create and save user-defined workspaces to fit various projects' design needs and your work style.

OPEN OR CLOSE A PANEL OR GROUP

The workspace saves which panels are open.

- To open a panel that's not already displayed, choose its name from the Window menu. The panel will appear in its default group on the dock or in its most recent open location.

- To bring a panel to the front of its group, click its tab.

- To close a panel or group, right-click the panel icon or tab, and from the **context menu**, choose Close or Close Tab Group.

TIP

Press Tab to hide/ show all currently open panels.

EXPAND OR COLLAPSE A PANEL OR A DOCK

To expand a panel that's displaying as only an icon in a dock, click its icon. To collapse an expanded panel back to an icon, click its icon again.

To collapse a panel or an entire dock (**Figure 1.14**), at the top of the panel or dock, click the Collapse to Icons button (▸▸). Click the same double arrow icon to expand an entire dock (**Figure 1.15**).

*Drag the left edge of a collapsed dock to display its panel names and icons (**Figure 1.16**).*

Figure 1.14 The collapsed dock

Figure 1.15 The expanded dock

Figure 1.16 Drag the left edge of the collapsed dock to display panel names.

For some panels (such as Color, Stroke, and Character) you can display some or all option areas by clicking the vertical arrow two or three times on the panel tab.

REARRANGE PANELS AND DOCKS

A panel can be repositioned even when its dock is collapsed. Drag the panel icon into or between another collapsed panel group on the dock (designated by a dark gray bar at its top) and use the drop zone indicators to determine the new position.

To arrange panels as you would like them in the workspace:

- To widen an expanded panel or dock, drag its side or bottom edge.
- To move a panel within its group, drag its tab left or right.
- To move a panel out of its group in the dock, drag its tab into a new group (**Figure 1.17**) or between panel groups, and release the mouse button when the blue drop zone border or line appears.
- To float an individual panel, drag its icon or tab out of a dock. Drag its tab back into the dock (and use the drop zone indicators) to redock the panel.

Figure 1.17 Dragging a panel into a new group on the dock. Note the blue drop zone border.

Figure 1.18 Dragging a panel to create a new dock

Figure 1.19 The panel in the newly created dock

To create a new vertical dock for panels, drag a panel tab or icon over the vertical left edge of the dock (**Figure 1.18**) and release the mouse button when the blue vertical drop zone bar appears (**Figure 1.19**). Drag other panel tabs or icons into the new vertical dock, as desired.

Save a Custom Workspace

Once you have customized your Illustrator workspace, you can save it for future use.

1 On the Application bar, from the workspace switcher menu, choose New Workspace.

2 In the New Workspace dialog box, enter a descriptive name for the workspace.

3 Click OK. Any user-defined workspaces you save will be listed at the top of the workspace switcher menu.

You can now switch between your user-defined workspace and any of the pre-defined Illustrator workspaces without losing your custom arrangement.

> **TIP** *To save any further changes to a custom workspace, from the workspace switcher menu, choose New Workspace. Enter the original workspace name and click OK to save the new changes to the existing workspace.*

NOTE

Use the Manage Workspaces command, accessed from the workspace switcher menu, to rename or delete a custom workspace.

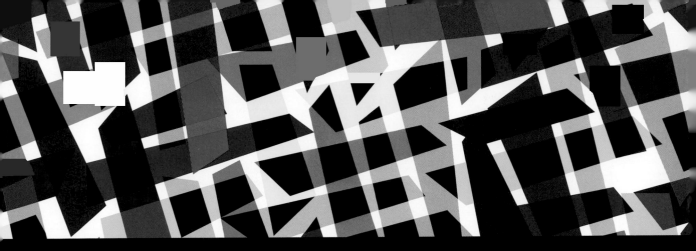

CHAPTER OBJECTIVES

Chapter Learning Objectives

- Create a new document.
- Work with artboards.
- Save a document.
- Navigate the Illustrator interface.
- End a work session.

Chapter ACA Objectives

DOMAIN 3.0
UNDERSTANDING ADOBE ILLUSTRATOR CC

3.3 Navigate, organize, and customize the workspace.

3.4 Use non-printing design tools in the interface, such as rulers, guides, bleeds, and artboards.

DOMAIN 4.0
CREATING DIGITAL GRAPHICS AND ILLUSTRATIONS USING ADOBE ILLUSTRATOR CC

4.1 Create a new project.

DOMAIN 5.0
ARCHIVE, EXPORT, AND PUBLISH GRAPHICS USING ADOBE ILLUSTRATOR CC

5.2 Export digital graphics and illustration to various file formats.

CHAPTER 2

Working with Documents

You're ready to create your own Illustrator document. In this chapter, you will create a new document, work with the artboards in the document, and save that document.

NOTE

This chapter supports the Video Intro. Go to the Video Intro page in the book's Web Edition to watch the entire video intro from beginning to end.

Create a Document

★ *ACA Objective 4.1*

Illustrator documents display within the Application frame as tabbed windows. The document's name is listed in its tab. Each document contains at least one artboard. You can modify the number and arrangement of artboards within your new document at any time after you create a document.

 *Video Intro 02*
Create a New Document

Create a New Document

To get started on creating artwork in Illustrator, you'll first create a new document.

1   Choose File > New. The New Document dialog box opens (**Figure 2.1**).

2   Enter a name for the new document in the Name field.

3   From the Profile menu, choose a profile that matches the output medium for which you are designing. For this exercise, choose Print.

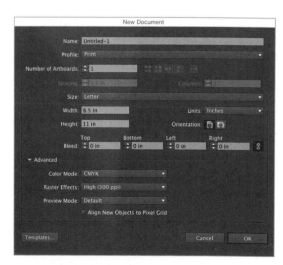

Figure 2.1 The New Document dialog box

4   Every Illustrator document must contain at least one artboard (see the next section for more on artboards). For this exercise, leave the setting at the default of 1.

5   From the Size menu, choose a preset that matches your project. For this exercise, choose Letter.

6   Click the first Orientation button to specify that the artboard is in portrait orientation (rather than landscape orientation).

> **NOTE** *You can specify a **bleed** area to accommodate objects that need to print to the edge of a printed piece. Bleed values can be entered in the New Document dialog box, the Document Setup dialog box, or the Print dialog box. When you use the Bleed fields, be sure the Make All Settings the Same button is enabled (darkened) to uniformly modify all the fields.*

7   Expand the Advanced settings area, if necessary, and view the default settings for the Print profile you selected. (Notice that the default color mode for Print is CMYK.) Leave the settings as they are now.

8   Click OK. A new document window opens (**Figure 2.2**).

9   To place an object on your new document, display the Symbols panel, and drag any symbol onto the artboard.

Figure 2.2 The elements in the Illustrator document window

Artboards

Every Illustrator document contains at least one **artboard** of the dimensions speci-fied in the New Document dialog box. The artboard is called the "live" area because any objects placed on that artboard will output to your chosen output device or be exported with your final file.

A document can have multiple artboards of a uniform size or of different sizes. For example, you could create a document with customized artboards that each contain a business card, stationery, or a brochure for a client identity package, or a docu-ment with separately sized web graphics for a website project.

Using the Illustrator Artboard tool ⊞, you can edit your artboards at any time. When you choose this tool, you enter Artboard mode and can manage your art-boards. The Control panel will display settings and options related to artboards. To exit Artboard mode, press Esc or select a different tool.

★ ACA Objective 3.4

Add Artboards

You can add additional artboards to a document at any time.

1 Select the Artboard tool icon ⊞ or press Shift+O.

2 On the View menu, select Smart Guides to show onscreen alignment guides.

3 Hold the Command key (Mac OS) or Ctrl key (Windows) and press – (hyphen) to zoom out and view more of the canvas area in your document.

4 Using the Artboard tool, drag in the canvas to create a new artboard (**Figure 2.3**). Use the smart guides to help align the new artboard with an existing one.

TIP

To quickly place an object in your docu-ment onto all of the artboards, click the object with the Selec-tion tool (V), choose Edit > Copy, and then choose Edit > Paste On All Artboards.

Figure 2.3 Using the Artboard tool to add an artboard to a document

Resize Artboards

Options on the Control panel enable you to fine-tune the size of a selected artboard (**Figures 2.4** and **2.5**).

- Click an artboard to select it.
- Select a screen or paper size from the Presets menu.
- Enter values in the W and H fields.
- Select a different Orientation button.

You can also resize a selected artboard by dragging a corner or side handle.

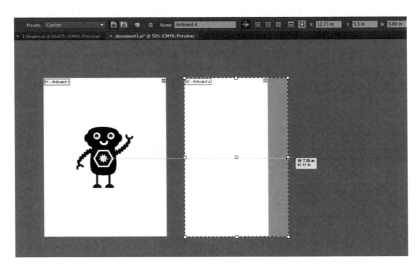

Figure 2.4 Resizing the artboard

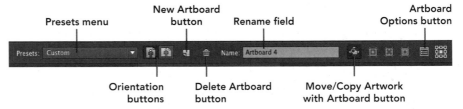

Figure 2.5 The Control panel in Artboard mode

Presets menu   New Artboard button   Rename field   Artboard Options button

Orientation buttons   Delete Artboard button   Move/Copy Artwork with Artboard button

Duplicate an Artboard

The Artboards panel and the Artboard tool enable you to duplicate an artboard in a document, with or without its contents.

DUPLICATE WITHOUT THE CONTENTS

To duplicate a selected artboard without its contents:

- **Using the Artboards panel:** On the Artboards panel, click a listing to select the artboard you want to duplicate. Click the New Artboard button ▣. The blank, duplicate artboard is added to the right of the existing artboards.

- **Using the Artboard tool:** Select the Artboard tool (or press Shift+O). On the Control panel, click to deactivate the Move/Copy Artwork With Artboard button ✥. Option-drag (Mac OS) or Alt-drag (Windows) the artboard you want to duplicate.

- **Using the Artboard tool:** Select the Artboard tool (or press Shift+O) and select the artboard to duplicate. On the Control panel, click the New Artboard button. Position the Artboard tool pointer on the canvas (use smart guides for alignment), and click to create the duplicate artboard.

DUPLICATE WITH THE CONTENTS

To duplicate a selected artboard with its contents:

- **Using the Artboards panel:** On the Artboards panel, click a listing to select the artboard you want to duplicate. Drag the selected listing to the New Artboard button ▣. The duplicate artboard with contents is added to the right of the existing artboards.

- **Using the Artboard tool:** Select the Artboard tool (or press Shift+O). On the Control panel, click to activate the Move/Copy Artwork With Artboard button. Option-drag (Mac OS) or Alt-drag (Windows) the artboard you want to duplicate (**Figure 2.6**).

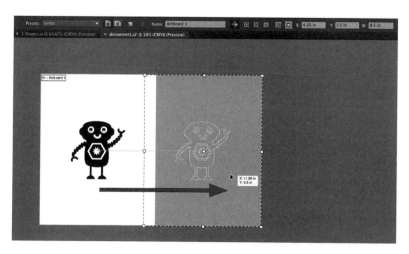

Figure 2.6 Duplicating an artboard

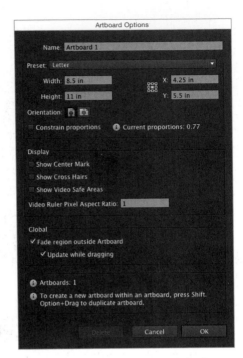

Figure 2.7 The Artboard Options dialog box

Delete an Artboard

When you delete an artboard, you will not delete its contents. Do one of the following:

- **Using the Artboards panel:** On the Artboards panel, click the listing for the artboard you want to delete, and then click the Delete Artboard button ![trash icon].

- **Using the Artboard tool:** Select the Artboard tool. In the upper-right corner of a selected artboard, click the Delete icon, or press Delete (Mac OS) or Backspace (Windows) on the keyboard.

- **Using the Artboard Options dialog box (Figure 2.7):** In addition to using the Control panel, Artboards panel, and Artboard tool, you can modify the selected artboard (including deleting the artboard) using the Artboard Options dialog box. To open it, click the Artboard Options button on the Control panel. The Artboard Options dialog box is useful for changing many artboard attributes at the same time.

★ *ACA Objective 5.2*

Save a Document

▶ *Video Intro 04*
Save a Document

You can save an Illustrator file in six different formats, although we will focus on the Adobe Illustrator (.ai) format in this exercise. Use the .ai format when you plan to print the file directly from Illustrator or when you plan to import the file into a program that can read the .ai format, such as Adobe InDesign.

TIP

Get in the habit of saving often so you don't accidentally lose any recent edits.

1. To save a document for the first time, choose File > Save, or press Command+S (Mac OS) or Ctrl+S (Windows).

2. In the Save As (Mac OS) or File Name (Windows) field, enter a filename.

3. Navigate to the desired save folder.

4. From the Format (Mac OS) or Save as Type (Windows) menu, choose the Adobe Illustrator (.ai) format.

5. Click Save.

   The Illustrator Options dialog box opens (**Figure 2.8**).

6 Leave the Version menu set to Illustrator CC.

7 Verify that Create PDF Compatible File is selected under Options.

Illustrator saves a PDF version (along with the Illustrator data) that will allow applications that can't read Illustrator data to open and display the file.

8 Select Embed ICC Profiles to embed any **color profile** assigned to the file.

9 Select Use Compression to reduce the saved file's size.

10 Click OK. The file is saved and will remain open in Illustrator. Keep your document open and proceed to the next task.

> **TIP** *After naming and saving a document for the first time, press Command+S (Mac OS) or Ctrl+S (Windows) to save any further edits to the file.*

> **TIP** *Choose File > Save As to save a variation of an existing file. Change the name in the name field (as described in step 2 earlier), and then perform the remaining steps.*

Figure 2.8 The Illustrator Options dialog box opens when you save a new document.

Navigating the Illustrator Interface

★ *ACA Objective 3.3*

It's important to know how to arrange multiple documents within the interface; how to view and zoom in on specific areas of a document; and how to view your artwork in a clean, panel-free screen view. You will do these things often as you work and as you show your work to others.

Arrange Multiple Document Windows

In the Application frame, you can tile multiple documents in various layouts, such as side-by-side or vertically stacked.

1 Open the Shapes1.ai and Shapes2.ai documents in the Intro-01 Workarea folder.

2 In the Application bar, select an option from the Arrange Documents menu (**Figure 2.9**). The number of available arrangement icons varies depending on the number of open documents.

Figure 2.9 The Arrange
Documents menu on the
Application bar

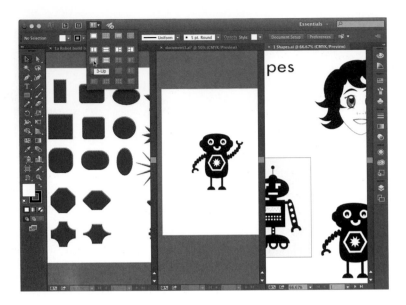

3 Click within a tiled window to select it. Click the Hand tool (or press H) to
    select it, and then drag in any tiled window to reposition the view.

4 To redisplay only one document window, select Consolidate All from the
    Arrange Documents menu (**Figure 2.10**).

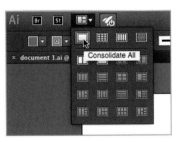

Figure 2.10 Working with
multiple document windows

Document Tabs

Each open document displays a tab below the Application bar. The tab lists the document name, zoom level, color mode (CMYK or RGB), and view (Outline, Preview,
or Overprint Preview).

Click a document's tab to make that file the active document. Right-click a tab to
display various document commands in a context menu.

Change the Zoom Level

As you create and modify artwork in a document, you may need to zoom in to view more details or zoom out to view the entire artwork.

- **Zoom in:** To zoom in, hold Command (Mac OS) or Ctrl (Windows) and press + (plus sign) repeatedly until you're zoomed in as far as you want.

- **Zoom out:** To zoom out, hold Command (Mac OS) or Ctrl (Windows) and press - (hyphen) repeatedly until you're zoomed out as far as you want.

- **Percentage:** In the zoom menu in the lower-left corner of the document window, choose a preset percentage to zoom or enter a value in the zoom field and press Return (Mac OS) or Enter (Windows).

- **Fit document in window:** From the View menu, choose Fit Artboard in Window, or press Command+0 (zero) (Mac OS) or Ctrl+0 (zero) (Windows) to fill the document window with the active artboard.

- **Fit artboards in window:** From the View menu, choose Fit All in Window to fit all the artboards within the document window.

- **Zoom tool:** Select the Zoom tool ⚲ on the Tools panel (or press Z), and click to zoom in. To zoom out, Option-click (Mac OS) or Alt-click (Windows).

TIP *If GPU Performance acceleration is enabled, select the Zoom tool and drag to the right to zoom in or drag to the left to zoom out. You will know that GPU Performance is enabled when the GPU Performance "rocket" icon is enabled on the Application bar and GPU Preview displays in the document tabs. Click the rocket icon to access the GPU Performance panel in the Preferences dialog box and turn the feature on/off.*

Using the Status Bar

The **status bar** and its menu are located in the lower-left quadrant of the document window. The bar displays information for the category that you have selected from the Show submenu of the status bar. Helpful options include Artboard Name, Current Tool, and Number of Undos (**Figure 2.11**).

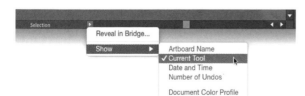

Figure 2.11 The status bar on the document window

View Different Areas of a Document

After you zoom in to view a portion of your artwork, you can select the Hand tool 🖐, and drag to pan across the document and bring a different document area or artboard into view. To quickly access the Hand tool, press H to select it or hold down the spacebar to use it temporarily. To quickly move between artboards, do one of the following:

- In the Artboards panel, double-click to the right of an artboard listing to quickly fit that artboard into the document window.

- From the **artboard navigation** menu in the lower left of the document window, choose a number; or click the First, Previous, Next, or Last arrow to quickly move between multiple artboards.

Changing the Screen Mode

To view your artwork without the distractions of the surrounding panels or your desktop, switch to the full screen modes. To do this, you can press F several times to cycle through the three screen modes or select an option from the Screen Mode menu at the bottom of the Tools panel (**Figure 2.12**):

- **Normal Screen Mode** displays the document in the Application frame with all the panels. This is the default mode.

- **Full Screen Mode with Menu Bar** displays a document in the Application frame with the panels, but without showing document tabs.

- **Full Screen Mode** displays the document in a maximized window with all panels hidden.

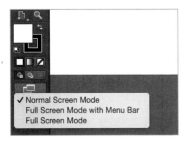

Figure 2.12 The Screen Mode menu at the bottom of the Tools panel

Ending a Work Session

To finish a work session in Illustrator:

1 Save and close each document that's open:

   ■ To close each document, click the X on the document tab next to the file-name or press Command+W (Mac OS) or Ctrl+W (Windows).

   ■ If the document contains unsaved changes, an alert displays. Click Save to preserve changes or Don't Save to discard the latest changes.

2 When all the documents are closed, choose Illustrator > Quit Illustrator (Mac OS) or File > Exit (Windows). You can also press Command+Q (Mac OS) or Ctrl+Q (Windows).

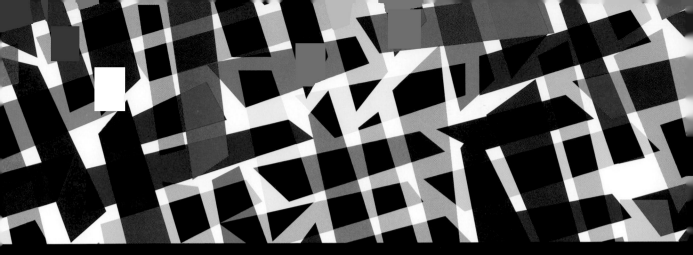

CHAPTER OBJECTIVES

Chapter Learning Objectives

- Create basic geometric shapes.
- Reshape a corner via live shapes and live corners.
- Move a corner point.
- Remove a point.

Chapter ACA Objectives

DOMAIN 3.0
UNDERSTANDING ADOBE ILLUSTRATOR CC

3.2 Define the functions of commonly used tools, including selection tools, the Pen tool, and other drawing tools, shape tools, and transformation tools.

DOMAIN 4.0
CREATING DIGITAL GRAPHICS AND ILLUSTRATIONS USING ADOBE ILLUSTRATOR CC

4.2 Use vector drawing and shape tools.

4.3 Transform graphics and illustrations.

CHAPTER 3

Creating Basic Shapes

In this chapter, you will create basic shapes, and modify the corners of the shapes. In the process, you will start to create your own custom shapes.

Basic Geometric Shapes

In Illustrator CC, you use the drawing tools on the Tools panel to create shapes. A shape is a path that consists of straight and/or curved line segments connected by anchor points. The path on a shape can be open (as in a line or a spiral), or closed (as in a circle, which has no starting and ending point). Any created element in an Illustrator document is also referred to as an object.

> **REMOVING THOSE LESS-THAN-SUCCESSFUL DRAWN OBJECTS**
>
> When using the drawing tools, it's easy to fill your artboard with unwanted junk. To remove an unwanted object, click it with the Selection tool. Press Delete (Mac OS) or Backspace (Windows) to remove the selection.

Create Geometric Shapes

First, let's create some basic geometric shapes.

1. Create a new document by choosing File > New.
2. In the New Document dialog box, select Print from the Profile menu.
3. In the Number of Artboards field, type **3**.
4. Select Letter from the Size menu. Specify any other desired settings, and click OK.

★ *ACA Objective 4.2*

TIP

When editing objects (applying color, moving an object, adjusting a corner point, and so on), to remove your last edit, choose Edit > Undo or press Command+Z (Mac OS) or Ctrl+Z (Windows) immediately. Repeat the command to step back through prior edits and remove them. Remember the keyboard shortcut for the Undo feature; you will use it quite often in Illustrator.

NOTE

This chapter supports the project created in Video Project 01. Go to the Video Project 01 page in the book's Web Edition to watch the entire project from beginning to end.

5 Select the Rectangle tool (M)  or the Ellipse tool (L) 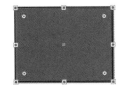.

6 Drag diagonally across an artboard, and release the mouse button.

A rectangle or oval shape is created with the current fill and stroke settings applied to it (**Figure 3.1**). Once you create an object, it remains selected so you can make additional changes to it.

7 Draw several more rectangles and ellipses on the artboard. When you're finished, choose File > Save As to name and save your document. Leave it open.

Figure 3.1 Drag to create and fill a rectangle shape as shown.

DRAW PERFECT SQUARES AND CIRCLES

To draw a square or circle, Shift-drag with the Rectangle tool, Rounded Rectangle tool, or Ellipse tool.

To draw a shape from its center, Option-drag (Mac OS) or Alt-drag (Windows) using any shape tool.

Create a Rounded Rectangle

Illustrator provides a handy tool to create a rectangle with rounded corners.

1 Select the Rounded Rectangle tool .

2 Drag diagonally across an artboard, and release the mouse button.

A rounded rectangle shape is created with the current fill and stroke settings applied to it (**Figure 3.2**).

Figure 3.2 A rounded rectangle shape created with the current fill and stroke settings

Create Other Basic Shapes

The Rectangle tool and Line Segment tool both provide access to various hidden tools that enable you to create other basic shapes. Remember, once you create a shape, the current fill and stroke settings are applied and the shape remains selected for further modifications.

CREATE A POLYGON

You can create a polygon by dragging or clicking with the Polygon tool.

1 Select the Polygon tool ⬡.

2 Place the pointer where you want to locate the center of the shape and drag across an artboard. While dragging, do any of the following:

   ■ To scale the polygon, drag away from or toward the center.

   ■ To rotate the polygon, drag in a circular direction.

   ■ To add sides to or remove sides from the polygon, press the Up and Down Arrow keys (**Figures 3.3** and **3.4**).

3 Release the mouse button. The polygon shape is selected.

TIP

To create a polygon by entering values, click the Polygon tool on an artboard. In the dialog box that opens, enter Radius and Sides values, and click OK.

Figure 3.3 A polygon shape with six sides

Figure 3.4 A polygon shape with nine sides

CREATE A STAR

You can create a star by dragging or clicking with the Star tool.

1 Select the Star tool ⭐.

2 Locate the pointer where your want to locate the center of the shape, and drag across an artboard. While dragging, do any of the following:

   ■ To scale the star, drag away from or toward the center.

   ■ To rotate the star, drag in a circular direction.

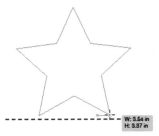

Figure 3.5 Points constrained on horizontal axis

Figure 3.6 Points added to star shape

Figure 3.7 Arms lengthened on star shape

- To constrain two points of the star to the horizontal axis, Shift-drag (**Figure 3.5**).

- To add points to or remove points from the star, press the Up and Down Arrow keys (**Figure 3.6**).

- To lengthen or shorten the arms of the star, Command-drag (Mac OS) or Ctrl-drag (Windows) away from or toward the center of the star (**Figure 3.7**).

3 Release the mouse button to create the star shape.

> **TIP** *To create a star by entering values, click the Star tool on an artboard. In the dialog box that opens, enter Radius 1 and 2 values. The higher value creates the outermost points. The greater the difference between the two radius values, the narrower the arms will be. Next, enter a Points value to specify the number of points on the star, and click OK.*

CREATE A LINE SEGMENT

The Line segment tool is the easiest way to draw a straight line.

1 Select the Line Segment tool /.

2 Drag to draw a straight line. Shift-drag to constrain the line to the horizontal axis, vertical axis, or a 45° angle.

3 Release the mouse button to create the line segment.

> **NOTE** *If your line segment has a stroke of white color, or a small stroke weight, it may be hard to see. See "Working with Fill and Stroke" in Chapter 4 to learn how to edit the color.*

> **TIP**
>
> *To create a line segment by entering values, click the Line Segment tool where you want the line to begin. In the dialog box, enter a Length value and an Angle value, and click OK.*

CREATE A TRIANGLE

You can create a triangle by modifying a polygon object.

1 Select the Polygon tool and click a blank area of an artboard. In the Polygon dialog box, in the Sides field, type **3**. Click OK.

   You now have a three-cornered object.

2 Use the Direct Selection (A) tool to drag any of the three corner points to reshape the triangle.

Reshape a Corner

★ *ACA Objective 3.2*

The simplest way to reshape an object is to use the Live Shapes and Live Corners features to modify the corners of the path. These two features enable you to easily created rounded segments on one or all of the corners on a shape. The features are "live" because you can adjust or even remove the curvature of a corner point at any time.

▶ *Video Project*
01-01 *Basic Shape—Live Shapes*

CREATE A COPY USING THE SELECTION TOOL

To preserve your original geometric shape, you can create a copy of the object and reshape the copy.

1 Select the Selection tool.

2 Option-drag (Mac OS) or Alt-drag (Windows) to copy an object and reposition the copy.

RESHAPE THE CORNERS OF A PATH USING LIVE SHAPES

You can apply the **Live Shapes** feature to a rectangle or rounded rectangle when all the points on the object are selected. Live Shapes (and its widgets) will remain active for these types of objects even if you scale or rotate the objects.

1 Select the Selection tool. Do one of the following:

   ■ Click inside a rectangle or a rounded rectangle object that displays a fill color.

   ■ Click the path (edge) of a rectangle or a rounded rectangle object that has a fill of None.

   Corner widgets will appear inside each corner of the selected shape.

2   Choose Window > Transform to open the Transform panel.

When a rectangle or rounded rectangle is selected, the middle portion of the panel displays the Rectangle (shape) Properties settings. These shape settings, along with the corner widgets, make up the Live Shapes feature.

3   Do any of the following:

- Drag a corner widget inward (**Figure 3.8**) to adjust the corner radius for all of the corners (**Figure 3.9**). (Remember, the entire object is selected.) To change the corner style, Option-click (Mac OS) or Alt-click (Windows) any widget to cycle through the three corner styles (round, inverted, or chamfer).

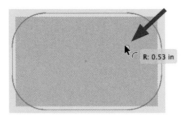

Figure 3.8 Drag a corner widget inward.

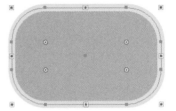

Figure 3.9 All the corners are modified uniformly.

TIP

When a rectangle object is selected, you can click the underlined word Shape on the Control panel to display the Rectangle (shape) properties settings on a temporary Transform panel.

- In the Transform panel, in the Rectangle Properties area, click any arrow to adjust the corner radius. When the Link Corner Radius Values button ⊠ is enabled, all the corners are modified. You can click the Link button to disable it, and adjust the corner radius value for a single corner (**Figures 3.10** and **3.11**).

Figure 3.10 On the Transform panel, with the Link Corner Radius Values button disabled, a single corner can be modified.

Figure 3.11 The resulting object with the corner changed

- In the Transform panel, click one of the four Corner Type menus, and select the Round, Inverted Round, or Chamfer button to modify the style for that corner only.

RESHAPE A SINGLE CORNER USING LIVE CORNERS

The Live Corners feature is enabled for reshaped rectangle objects and other polygon objects. It is most effective when used on an individually selected corner point or curve segment.

▶ **Video Project 01-03** *Basic Shape—Live Corners*

1 Select the Direct Selection tool (A) ▸.

2 Click inside a nonrectangular or noncurved shape (that has a fill color) to select all of the corner points on its path and display the individual widgets. Once you see how all the selected corners look, click outside the shape to deselect it.

3 Click a corner anchor point or the curved segment of a corner. Only the widget for that corner will display.

4 Do any of the following:

   ▪ Drag the widget inward or outward to adjust the corner radius (**Figure 3.12**).

Figure 3.12 Drag the widget to modify the corner radius.

   ▪ Option-click (Mac OS) or Alt-click (Windows) the widget to cycle through the three corner styles (round, inverted, or chamfer).

   ▪ Double-click the widget (or click the underlined word "Corners" in the Control panel) to open the Corners dialog box. Change the Radius value and/or the Corner style setting (**Figure 3.13**). Click OK.

TIP

When you drag the corner widget inward to its maximum amount, the curved segment is highlighted in red. The maximum curve highlight indicator will also display when dragging all the widgets inward using the Live Shapes feature.

 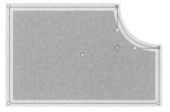

Figure 3.13 A corner was changed to the inverted round style.

Move a Corner

At this point, you have created simple geometric shapes and adjusted the curvature of the corners on those shapes. Now, you will learn how to reposition and remove anchor points to reshape an object's path.

It's time to take a closer look at the components of a path. Simply put, a path is composed of anchor points connected by line segments. An anchor point can be either a corner point connecting two straight line segments or a curved point connecting one or two curved line segments.

Move a Corner Point

You can drag an anchor point to reshape its path.

NOTE

Dragging a corner anchor point of a rectangle object will disable the Live Shapes feature, but will not disable the Live Corners feature.

1 Choose View > Smart Guides. (If a check mark is displayed, the feature is already enabled.)

2 Use the Rectangle tool, the Polygon tool, and the Star tool to create some basic object shapes. Apply a fill and stroke color to each object.

3 Using the Direct Selection tool, locate the pointer over a corner point on one of the objects that you created in step 2. A white anchor point indicator appears. Drag the point to reshape the path (**Figure 3.14**).

Figure 3.14 Drag a corner point to reposition it. The corner point still displays a widget.

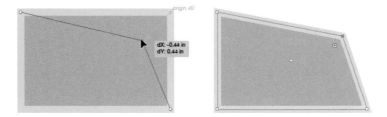

NOTE

Live Corners (and its widget) will remain active unless you lengthen or shorten either direction handle.

4 Drag the corner widget for the selected anchor point inward (**Figure 3.15**). You now have two anchor points connected by a curved segment (**Figure 3.16**). Each point will also have a direction handle.

- You can drag the widget back into the corner to remove the curve and restore the single corner anchor point or drag the curve segment outward to create a bump on the path (and remove the corner widget).

- Remember to use the Undo command if you want to restore the corner widget.

5 Experiment with moving anchor points on the other basic objects.

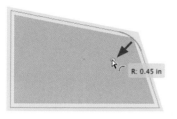

Figure 3.15 Drag the widget inward to add direction handles to the corner.

Figure 3.16 Moving a direction handle removes the inside corner widget.

Remove a Point

You can remove (delete) an anchor point from the path of any Illustrator object. In the following steps, you will create a triangle by simply removing a corner point from a rectangle.

1 Select a rectangle object.

2 Do one of the following:

- Select the Pen tool (P). Locate the pointer over a corner point on the rectangle, and click to remove the point (**Figure 3.17**).

- Select the Direct Selection tool (A), and click an anchor point. On the Control panel, click Remove Selected Anchor Point .

Using either of these methods, the closed path will not be cut (meaning it will not become an open path).

You now have a three-corner object.

3 Use the Direct Selection (A) tool to drag any of the segments or corner points to reshape the object.

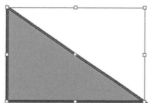

Figure 3.17 Click the Pen tool on a point to remove it.

★ *ACA Objective 4.3*

TIP
You can also remove a point using the Delete Anchor Point tool. To select this tool, press hyphen (–) or click and hold on the Pen tool to display the hidden tools and select it. Position the Delete Anchor Point tool over an anchor point on a selected or unselected object, then click. The tool will not open a closed path.

CHAPTER OBJECTIVES

Chapter Learning Objectives

- Work with Fill and Stroke.
- Apply gradients and patterns to fill and stroke.
- Use Recolor Art to change colors in multiple objects.
- Use Transform Again to produce copies.

Chapter ACA Objectives

DOMAIN 3.0
UNDERSTANDING ADOBE ILLUSTRATOR CC

3.6 Manage colors, swatches, and gradients.

CHAPTER 4

Fill, Stroke, and Color

In this chapter, you will learn how to apply color and patterns to basic shapes. You will combine skills learned in this chapter with the skills you learned in Chapter 3 to create your own custom shapes and assemble them into a recognizable image—a robot.

Working with Fill and Stroke

★ ACA Objective 3.6

▶ **Video Project 01-02** *Basic Shape—Fill and Stroke*

You can apply a variety of attributes to every object drawn in Illustrator. The two most basic attributes are the fill color (inside color) and stroke color (edge color) of the object's path. The stroke can have other settings to control its attributes, such as the width and exact placement of the color on the path.

Change the Fill and Stroke Color

You can modify the color of your newly created shapes at any time. You can use the following methods to change the fill and stroke colors.

APPLY COLORS VIA THE COLOR PANEL

1 Using the Selection tool ▶ (V), click an object in your document to select it.

2 On the Color panel, select a color model from the panel menu:

- To define colors for print output, select CMYK (**Figure 4.1**). In this case, your Illustrator document should have an output profile for print. You can define specific **process colors** in this color model.

- To define colors for video, web, or mobile device output, select RGB.

- To specify a shade of gray, select Grayscale.

NOTE

This chapter supports the project created in Video Project 01. Go to the Video Project 01 page in the book's Web Edition to watch the entire project from beginning to end.

TIP

To apply a fill or stroke of [None] to a selected object, click the [None] button 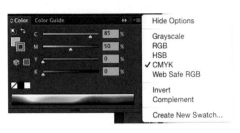 or press / (slash).

3 Click the Fill square. Drag the color sliders to mix a color, or click the color spectrum bar.

4 Click the Stroke square (or press X), and select a color using the color sliders or spectrum bar.

Figure 4.1 The Color panel

APPLY COLORS USING THE SWATCHES, CONTROL, OR APPEARANCE PANEL

You can also apply colors to objects by using the Swatches, Control, or Appearance panel.

1 Using the Selection tool ▶ (V), click an object in your document to select it.

2 Do any of the following:

TIP

To display a temporary Color panel from the Control or Appearance panel, Shift-click the Color square.

- On the Swatches panel, click the Fill square, and click a color swatch. Click the Stroke square (or press X), and click a color swatch (**Figure 4.2**).

- On the Control panel, click the Fill square or its menu, and on the temporary Swatches panel, click a color swatch. Click the Stroke square or its menu, and on the temporary Swatches panel, click a color swatch.

TIP

After using the color controls on the Control or Appearance panel, click anywhere in the document window to close the temporary Swatches or Color panel.

- On the Appearance panel, click the Fill listing, and click the Color square or its menu. On the temporary Swatches panel, click a color swatch. Click the Stroke listing, and click the Color square or its menu. On the temporary Swatches panel, click a color swatch (**Figure 4.3**).

- On any of these three panels, to apply a transparent fill or stroke, click the [None] swatch.

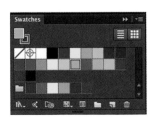

Figure 4.2 The Swatches panel

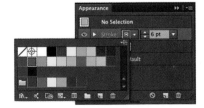

Figure 4.3 The Appearance panel

Apply Stroke Attributes

You can only see the stroke (edge) of a path if it has a weight applied. The weight is expressed in points. Once you can see the stroke, you can change how it aligns with the path, select caps for its endpoints, and change the corner style.

APPLY A STROKE WEIGHT

You can modify a path's stroke weight (width) using the Stroke, Control, or Appearance panel. Modifying the stroke weight on one of these panels updates the setting on the other two panels automatically.

1   Using the Selection tool ⬊ (V), click an object to select it.

2   Do either of the following:

   ▪ On the Stroke panel, enter a value in the Weight field or click the up and down arrows to increase or decrease the current stroke weight (**Figures 4.4** and **4.5**).

   ▪ On the Control panel, enter a value in the Stroke Weight field or click the up and down arrows to increase or decrease the current stroke weight.

TIP

You can change the stroke weight using the Appearance panel by clicking the Stroke listing to display a temporary Weight field, and clicking the up or down arrows to change the value.

TIP

On all three panels, click the down arrow next to the Weight field to display a menu of preset stroke weights. Click a value to select and apply it.

Figure 4.4 The Stroke panel

Figure 4.5 Stroke Weight changed

CHANGE THE STROKE ALIGNMENT

You can position a stroke on the inside, outside, or center of a path.

1   Using the Selection tool, click an object with a closed path (not a line) to select it.

2   Display all the areas on the Stroke panel by clicking the vertical arrow ⬍ on the panel tab two or three times.

3 Click the Align Stroke To Center, Align Stroke To Inside, or Align Stroke To Outside icon (**Figure 4.6**).

Figure 4.6 Align stroke to inside (left); align stroke to outside (right).

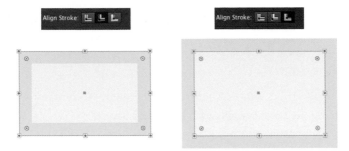

CHANGE THE STROKE CAP OR CORNER STYLE

You can apply different styles to the corners of a path (where it bends) and the endpoints on a line or open path (**Figure 4.7**).

1 Using the Selection tool, click an object to select it.

2 Display all the areas on the Stroke panel by clicking the vertical arrow on the panel tab.

3 To modify the corner points (not curved points) on a path, click one of the Corner icons:

- Miter Join creates a pointed corner.
- Round Join creates a rounded corner.
- Bevel Join creates a beveled (cut-off) corner.

4 To modify the endpoints on a line or open path, click one of the Cap icons:

- Butt Cap creates a square end.
- Round Cap creates a rounded end.
- Projecting Cap creates a square end that extends beyond each endpoint.

Figure 4.7 Path with a butt cap and miter corner (left); path with a round cap and round corner (right)

Apply Gradients and Patterns to Fills and Strokes

Applying a **gradient** or **pattern** to a selected object is a straightforward process. On the Swatches panel, click to make the Fill or Stroke square active, then click a gradient or pattern swatch on the panel to apply it.

NOTE

These attributes look best when applied to a wide stroke.

EXPLORE SWATCH LIBRARIES

If the Swatches panel does not currently display any gradient or pattern swatches, you will need to open a swatch library to add those types of swatches to the panel.

1 On the Swatches panel, click the Swatch Libraries menu 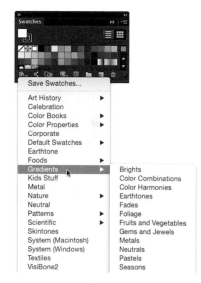. From the Gradients or Patterns submenu, select a library (**Figure 4.8**).

   A floating panel will open in the document window. The library name will appear in the panel tab (**Figure 4.9**).

2 Click a swatch or Shift-click multiple swatches. From the floating panel menu, select Add To Swatches to add the gradients or patterns to the Swatches panel.

3 Do one of the following:

   ▪ At the bottom of the panel, click the left or right arrow to display the previous or next swatch library that is listed on the Swatch Libraries menu and its submenus.

   ▪ On the floating panel, click the Swatch Libraries menu, and from the Gradients or Patterns (or any other category's) submenu, select another library. That library will display in the current floating panel or in a new floating panel.

   TIP *To close the floating panel, click the X in its upper-left corner.*

   TIP *You can drag floating panels into the dock.*

   NOTE *To make a library panel automatically reopen after quitting/ launching Illustrator, choose Persistent from the Library panel menu.*

Figure 4.8 Swatches panel library menu

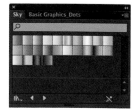

Figure 4.9 The Sky swatches library in the panel tab

Recolor Artwork

The Recolor Artwork command displays a dialog box of options for changing the colors on multiple selected objects. This feature provides a powerful way to change colors in an applied pattern, gradient, or solid color on selected objects.

1 Select one or more objects. Their fill and stroke can contain patterns, gradients, or solid colors.

2 On the Control panel, click the Recolor Artwork icon 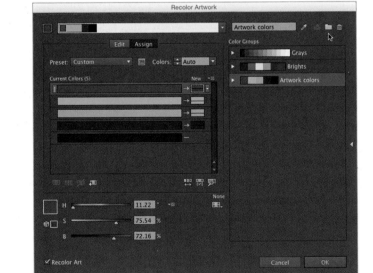.

3 In the lower part of the Recolor Artwork dialog box, select Recolor Art.

The following four sections explain how to use the Recolor Artwork dialog box.

SAVE THE EXISTING ARTWORK COLORS

In the Recolor Artwork dialog box, you can save the current colors applied to the objects (**Figure 4.10**).

1 In the top part of the dialog box, click the Get Colors From Selected Art dropper and enter a descriptive name in the Name field.

2 Click the New Color Group icon. A color group is added to the Color Groups list.

Figure 4.10 A new color group being added to the Color Groups list

ASSIGN NEW COLORS TO THE ARTWORK

The Recolor Artwork dialog box enables you to quickly change the colors applied to multiple selected objects.

1 On the left side of the dialog box, click the Assign tab. Colors from the selected objects appear in the Current Colors column.

2 With Recolor Art checked, do any of the following to recolor the selected art:

- In the Color Groups list, click a color group.

- Click a color in the New column, then drag the sliders below the Current Colors column.

- In the New column, double-click a color, and choose a new color in the Color Picker (**Figure 4.11**).

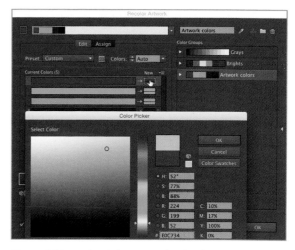

Figure 4.11 A color in the New column is being changed via the Color Picker.

EDIT COLORS USING THE COLOR WHEEL

You can modify existing colors with the color wheel in the Recolor Artwork dialog box (**Figure 4.12**).

1 Click the Edit tab at left. Colors from the selected artwork display as markers on a color wheel.

2 The Edit color wheel works as follows:

- If the black lines connecting the markers are dashed, click the Link Harmony Colors icon below the circle to create solid lines.

- Drag any marker to rotate all of the markers around the color wheel and shift the object colors. (Color harmonies are preserved.)

- Click the Harmony Color icon again to unlink colors and display dashed lines.

- Drag any marker to move it independently of the other markers and shift only that color (**Figure 4.13**).

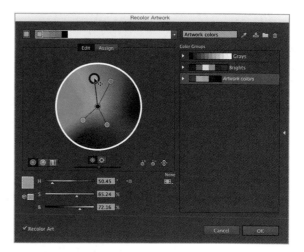

Figure 4.12 The Recolor Artwork dialog box

- Drag a marker inward or outward (or drag the S slider) to alter the saturation of only that color.
- Drag the slider immediately under the color wheel to alter the brightness of all the colors or drag the B slider to affect only the current marker.
- As an optional step, click either of the icons 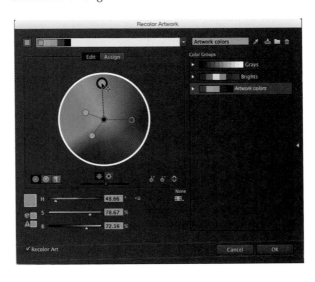 immediately below the wheel to toggle the slider (immediately below them) between altering the saturation or brightness for all of the artwork colors.

Figure 4.13 Shifting a single color

NOTE

If you do not like any of your color modifications, you can restore the original artwork colors by clicking the Get Colors From Selected Art dropper next to the Name field.

SAVE MODIFIED COLORS AS A COLOR GROUP

After modifying colors in the Recolor Artwork dialog box, you may save them as a group for later use.

1 Click the Name field in the upper right and enter a name for a new color group.

2 Click the New Color Group icon to the right of the field.

A new color group appears in the Color Groups list. Clicking this color group listing while the dialog box is still open will automatically reapply these colors to the artwork.

NOTE

Any new color groups you created in the Recolor Artwork dialog box are automatically added to the Swatches panel.

Apply the Modified Colors

When you are finished working in the Recolor Artwork dialog box, you can apply the modified colors to recolor the selected objects by clicking OK.

Arrange Basic Objects to Create a Robot

You can create oval and rectangular objects that can become the pieces for a recognizable shape—a robot head as shown in **Figure 4.14**. Using the shape tools, draw the large pieces first so that the smaller objects will be stacked in front of them.

▶ **Video Project** 01-04 *Basic Shape—Shapes for Robot*

Figure 4.14 Assembling the robot heads

TIP

If a larger object happens to be in front of the smaller objects, select the larger object and choose Object > Arrange > Send to Back to move it behind the smaller objects.

NOTE

You will learn how to restack objects using the Layers panel in the next chapter.

Create Multiple Copies Using Transform Again

To create a copy of and reposition selected objects, you can Option-drag (Mac OS) or Alt-drag (Windows). Then, you can use a command to quickly create and reposition additional copies. This method is much faster than dragging additional copies manually.

1 Select an object.

2 Option-drag (Mac OS) or Alt-drag (Windows) to create a copy. Leave the copy selected.

3 Choose Object > Transform > Transform Again. Alternatively, press Command+D (Mac OS) or Ctrl+D (Windows) press several times to make additional copies that are separated from each other by the amount you dragged in the previous step (**Figure 4.15**).

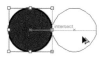 

Figure 4.15 Multiple copies created, and spaced as you specified

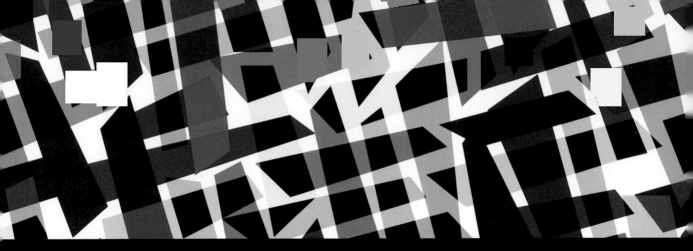

CHAPTER OBJECTIVES

Chapter Learning Objectives

- Learn about and compare selection tools.
- Draw a shape by reshaping and transforming basic objects.
- Explore more advanced reshaping.
- Reshape an oval to create custom objects.
- Transform objects to create variation.
- Learn about the Layers panel.

Chapter ACA Objectives

DOMAIN 3.0
UNDERSTANDING ADOBE ILLUSTRATOR CC

3.2 Define the functions of commonly used tools, including selection tools, the Pen tool, and other drawing tools, shape tools, and transformation tools.

3.5 Demonstrate knowledge of layers and masks.

DOMAIN 4.0
CREATING DIGITAL GRAPHICS AND ILLUSTRATIONS USING ADOBE ILLUSTRATOR CC

4.3 Transform graphics and illustrations.

4.4 Create and manage layers.

CHAPTER 5

Reshaping Objects

In this chapter, you will produce more complex artwork by reshaping objects. You will learn how to assemble recognizable images, such as faces, using a range of shapes created from basic objects. You will also transform a single object to quickly generate shapes of different sizes and orientation, and you will use the Layers panel to control the stacking order of objects in your artwork.

NOTE

This chapter supports the project created in Video Project 01. Go to the Video Project 01 page in the book's Web Edition to watch the entire project from beginning to end.

A Primer on Paths and Selection

Illustrator provides two main selection tools: the Selection tool and the Direct Selection tool. You will use these two tools more than any other tools in the Tools panel.

★ *ACA Objective 3.2*

Building Blocks of a Path

In Illustrator, all paths consist of segments that are connected by anchor points. There are two types of anchor points: smooth and corner.

A **smooth anchor point** connects two curved segments or a straight segment and a curved segment (**Figure 5.1**). Curved segments have **direction handles** that control the shape of the curve. The length of a direction handle controls the height of the curve. The angle of a direction handle controls the slope of the curve.

A **corner anchor point** connects two straight segments and therefore has no direction handles (**Figure 5.2**).

Figure 5.1 A smooth anchor point

Figure 5.2 A corner anchor point

Select or Transform an Entire Object

Use the Selection tool (V) ▸ to select or move an entire object or **group** as follows:

- Click inside an object with a visible fill to select it.
- Click the path (edge) of an object with a fill of [None] to select it.
- Drag across one or more objects to select them (a marquee indicates the selection area).
- Shift-click individual objects to add them to the current selection.

Once selected, a bounding box displays around the edge of that object (**Figure 5.3**) or around a selection of multiple objects.

- Drag a corner or side handle of the bounding box to scale the object (or objects).
- Drag a corner handle in a circular direction to rotate the object (or objects).

When you roll over an anchor point, the mouse pointer for each of the two selection tools displays a small square with a dot inside to identify the point.

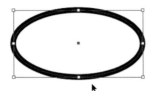

Figure 5.3 An entire object selected

When you position the Direct Selection tool over the path of an unselected object, a temporary white square reveals the location of an anchor point. To activate this feature, choose Illustrator > Preferences > Selection and Anchor Display (Mac OS) or Edit > Preferences > Selection and Anchor Display (Windows) and check Highlight Anchors on Mouse Over.

Select and Modify a Single Point

To change the shape of an object, you can move one or more points of that object.

1. Press A to select the Direct Selection tool ▹, and click one anchor point on a path to select it (**Figure 5.4**).

   If you click either a smooth anchor point or a curved segment on a path, the direction handles for that point or segment will display. Each handle controls the shape of the curved segment that extends from the point.

2. Modify the point by dragging it to reshape the object or modify a segment by dragging a direction handle.

Figure 5.4 A single anchor point selected

Draw a Face via Reshape and Transform

Now you're ready to produce a more elaborate illustration—a face created by combining simple ovals and circles. In the following task, you will reshape an oval object to create more hand-drawn, customized shapes that will add character to the face artwork.

▶ **Video Project**
01-05 Draw Faces via Reshape

Reshape an Oval to Make a Straight Hair Strand

You will make hair for this face from one repeated object. First, you will reshape the curved segments on an oval to produce the initial object, and then copy the object to create multiple hair strands.

1. Select the Ellipse tool (or press L), and draw a vertical oval.

2. Apply a gray fill and set the stroke to [None] for this object.

3. Select the Direct Selection tool (or press A). Select the bottommost anchor point on the oval object.

4. In the Control panel, click the Convert Selected Anchor Point To Corner button to convert the point into a corner point with straight segments (and no direction handles) (**Figure 5.5**).

5. Select the anchor point on the right side of the object. Drag the point (or press the Left Arrow key) to move it inward and flatten out the curvature of the right side of the oval (**Figure 5.6**).

6. Select the anchor point on the left side of the object. Drag it downward a bit (or press the Down Arrow key). Drag the anchor point's lower direction handle downward to lengthen the handle and reshape the curved segment (**Figure 5.7**).

7. Click the fill of the object to select the entire object. To create a copy, Option-drag (Mac OS) or Alt-drag (Windows) the vertical object.

8. Press Command+D (Mac OS) or Ctrl+D (Windows) about six times to apply the Transform Again command and create additional copies.

   You will use these copies in the next task.

Figure 5.5 Anchor point converted to corner point

Figure 5.6 Point moved inward

Figure 5.7 Curved segment reshaped

Transform Objects to Create Variation

★ ACA Objective 4.3 The reshaped oval can be transformed—scaled, rotated, or reflected—to create an object at a different size or orientation. Instead of redrawing an object, you can use transform features to modify a shape. Better still, the transform features can apply changes to a copy while preserving the original object.

You will use the objects that you previously created to construct the left and right symmetry of hair strands on the facial shape.

1   Use the Selection tool (V) to select a copy of the hair object.

2   Drag a corner handle on the object's bounding box to rotate the copy to fit along the curve of the left side of the face. Rotate the other copies to create a smooth progression from the vertical hair strand to an almost horizontal hair strand on the top left of the face (**Figure 5.8**).

Figure 5.8 Copies of the hair shape were rotated to fit one side of the face. A stroke was applied to the hair shapes to differentiate the individual objects.

3   After positioning the rotated objects on the left side of the face, Shift-click each object to select the hair strands.

4   Choose Object > Transform > Reflect.

5   In the Reflect dialog box, select Preview, click Vertical, and then click Copy. The selected objects are copied and reflected to fit the right side of the face.

6   Drag the selection to the right side of the face, and then deselect it (**Figure 5.9**).

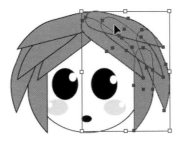

Figure 5.9 Objects copied and reflected to fit the right side of the face

Illustrator provides several ways to apply transformations (scale, rotate, reflect, and shear) to one or more selected objects. Vector objects that are transformed preserve the sharpness of their edges. This is one of the key advantages to using a vector drawing program such as Illustrator to create artwork.

You can choose one of the five transform commands on the Object > Transform submenu. An options dialog box will open in which you can choose settings and click Copy to create a transformed copy of your selected object.

You can also transform a selected object using its bounding box. Drag a corner handle to scale or rotate the object. Hold down Shift to either scale proportionately or rotate at 45° increments. Dragging a handle enables you to visually and interactively determine how much scaling or rotation to apply.

You can also choose a transform tool from the Tools panel. The Scale tool is grouped with the Shear tool , while the Rotate tool is grouped with the Reflect tool . You can drag any of these four tools to transform a selected object from its center. However, at this stage of your Illustrator training, it's probably easier to double-click the tool on the Tools panel to open its options dialog box (the same ones that you access from the Object > Transform submenu).

Draw a Second Face for an Advanced Reshape

The second face you will draw involves more advanced methods for reshaping oval objects and for stacking objects. These techniques create a more sophisticated character face.

Reshape an Oval to Make an Eyebrow

Once again, a simple oval is used as the starting shape to create several elements for the eye. To create an eyebrow, you will start by following the initial steps used to create the oval for the gray hair strand earlier.

1   Draw a vertical, black oval.

2. Use the Direct Selection tool (A) to select the bottommost anchor point. On the Control panel, click the Convert Selected Anchor Point To Corner button to convert the point into a corner point (**Figure 5.10**).

3. For the eyebrow shape, drag the anchor point on the right side of the object to move it inward and reverse the curvature of the right side of the oval (**Figure 5.11**).

4. Using the Selection tool (V), drag a corner handle on the object's bounding box to rotate the object to a horizontal orientation.

Figure 5.10 Anchor point converted to corner point

Reshape an Oval to Make an Eyelid

In these steps, you will apply short, straight segments to the ends of the oval.

1. Draw a horizontal oval. Apply a black fill and set the stroke to [None].

2. Using the Direct Selection tool (A), click the anchor point on one end of the object. Shift-click the point on the other end so that both points are selected.

3. On the Control panel, click the Convert Selected Anchor Point To Corner button to create two corner points (**Figure 5.12**).

Figure 5.11 Curvature reversed

4. At the top of the object, drag down the anchor point to reverse the curvature of the top part of the oval (**Figure 5.13**).

5. Zoom in on the object. Click the fill to select all of the points on the path, and then drag either live corner widget inward. The other widget will move in tandem because its point is also selected.

6. On the Control panel, click the Corners link. In the Corners dialog box, click the Chamfer (straight) button to create straight segments on the ends of the object (**Figure 5.14**).

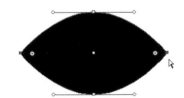

Figure 5.12 Two corner points created

Figure 5.13 Curve reversed

Figure 5.14 Creating new segments via the Corners dialog box

Reshape an Oval to Bend Its Curve

Let's experiment with bending the curve on a reshaped oval. You can work with a copy of the eyelid shape created in the prior task (**Figure 5.15**). Before starting, drag to create two additional copies of the eyelid shape.

1 Using the Direct Selection tool (A), drag the upper-left segment outward to reshape it (**Figure 5.16**).

Notice that the anchor points don't move, just the segment. While this method is easy, it limits the amount of curvature you can apply before the path becomes distorted. Let's try another method.

2 Press Command+Z (Mac OS) or Ctrl+Z (Windows) to undo the segment change.

3 This time, click the anchor point on the upper curve and drag its left direction handle upward and outward (**Figure 5.17**).

This method achieves the same, if not better, reshaping results. (Notice that a direction handle was not added to the corner point.)

4 On one of the copies, select the two curved points on the middle of the shape. Drag them upward and to the left to bend and "tilt" the curve to one side (**Figure 5.18**).

5 On one of the copies, drag a corner point downward to bend half of the path. Two direction handles in the middle of the shape should now be visible.

6 Rotate one of the two direction handles downward to smooth out its curve. Do the same for the direction handle on the other point (**Figure 5.19**).

TIP

Lengthening either of the direction handles on the center curve points will alter the thickness of the curved shape.

Figure 5.15 The original curve shape

Figure 5.16 Dragging out the curve

Figure 5.17 Curve dragged upward and outward

Figure 5.18 Curve tilted

Figure 5.19 Point dragged down

Reshape an Oval to Make a Facial Shape

For the second face, you will again modify anchor points and direction handles to create the bends and curves needed for a more elaborate facial shape.

1 Draw a vertical oval.

2 Using the Direct Selection tool (A), select the top anchor point. Drag the point downward to flatten the top of oval.

3 Drag each direction handle outward to lengthen it and make the top of the oval more like a rounded rectangle shape (**Figure 5.20**).

4 Select and drag each direction handle on the bottom point inward to shorten it and create a sharper (less smooth) curve at bottom of the shape (**Figure 5.21**).

5 Drag each side anchor point on the path outward slightly to widen the shape (**Figure 5.22**).

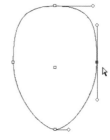

Figure 5.20 Top of the oval flattened

Figure 5.21 Sharper curve created at the bottom

Figure 5.22 Head widened

Reshape an Oval to Make a Wavy Hair Strand

The black hair strands for this face are produced by applying a different set of modifications to an oval object.

1 Draw a horizontal oval. Drag the anchor point on the right side of the oval upward (**Figure 5.23**).

2 Option-drag (Mac OS) or Alt-drag (Windows) the upper direction handle to rotate it into the object and reshape its curved segment.

3 Rotate the point's other direction handle outward to round out its curved segment (**Figure 5.24**).

You now have an object composed of smooth and non-smooth curves.

WORKING WITH A SMOOTH CURVE

In this exercise, you will work with a type of curved point called a smooth curve. As its name implies, its two segments create a continuous, symmetrical curve on either side of an associated anchor point. The direction handles for a smooth curve point always move in tandem to preserve the smoothness of the curve.

When you Option-drag (Mac OS) or Alt-drag (Windows) a direction handle on a smooth curve point, that handle will move independently of the other handle. The two curved segments will no longer create a continuous, smooth curve.

4 Drag both of the anchor points on the top and left of the object to the left. Experiment with rotating and changing the lengths of each point's direction handles to reshape the curved segments (**Figure 5.25**).

5 Select the entire object. Drag any of the side handles on the bounding box to modify the width and/or height of the object.

6 Create multiple copies of the object for use in the next task.

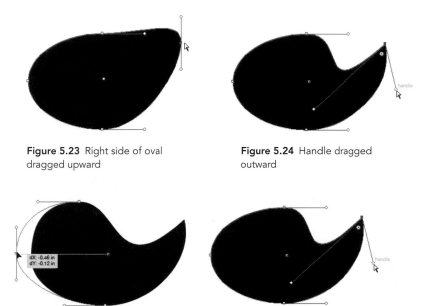

Figure 5.23 Right side of oval dragged upward

Figure 5.24 Handle dragged outward

Figure 5.25 Final adjustments to hair made

Transform Objects to Create Variation and Symmetry

You can use the same transform methods you learned previously to reorient the eyebrows, lids, lashes, and hair objects to fit properly on the left and right sides of the facial shape.

ASSEMBLE THE HAIR

You will arrange the multiple copies of the wavy hair strand to create the look of hair around the face object.

1 Rotate some of the copies of the hair object to orient the shapes to fit the top and sides of the face object (**Figure 5.26**).

2 Reflect some of the copies of the hair object to generate variations that you can place on the opposite side of the face object (**Figure 5.27**).

3 Shift-drag a corner handle on a hair object's bounding box to scale the shape down in size.

4 Drag a side handle to alter the width or height proportions of the object.

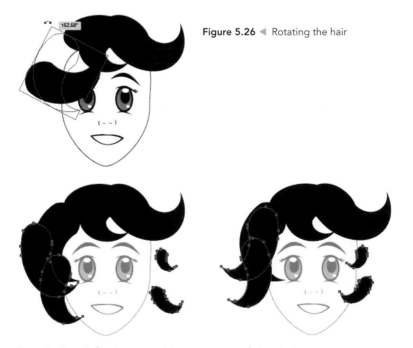

Figure 5.26 ◀ Rotating the hair

Figure 5.27 ▲ Reflecting some objects to generate hair variations

Layers Panel (First Look)

★ ACA Objective 3.5

★ ACA Objective 4.4

It's time to start placing your drawn objects in front of or behind each other to refine your character's face.

Create New Layers on the Layers Panel

When you create an object, it's automatically placed on the currently selected (active) layer. The front-to-back order of shapes in your artwork is determined by the top-to-bottom stacking order of the layers and nested layers listed in the Layers panel.

1 If necessary, choose Window > Layers to display the Layers panel.

2 Click the Create New Layer button 🔲 on the bottom of the panel two times (**Figure 5.28**).

Two new top-level layers are created. Top-level layers are always visible on the panel and can't be nested within other layers.

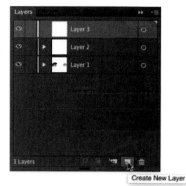

Figure 5.28 Creating two new layers in the Layers panel

Move Selected Objects to a New Layer

Drawing or placing all the objects in a document on one layer is not a good workflow practice. It's better to organize objects as a collection in specific top-level layers to make it easier to hide/show or select all of the objects on that layer.

1 On the Layers panel, click the disclosure triangle to the left of Layer 1 to expand its listing.

2 Using the Selection tool (V), click an object in the document. Shift-click other objects that create parts of your character shape.

On the Layers panel, small selection squares are displayed to the right of the <Path> listings for those objects. A small selection square also displays to the right of the top-level layer listing that contains the selected objects.

> **NOTE**
>
> *You can rename any layer by double-clicking its current name. Enter a new name, then press Return (Mac OS) or Enter (Windows).*

Figure 5.29 Moving the selection in the Layers panel

3   Do one of the following:

■   Drag each small selection square, one at a time, onto one of the new top-level layer listings.

■   Drag the small selection square on the top-level layer listing onto one of the new top-level layer listings to restack all of the selected objects with one move (**Figure 5.29**).

4   Repeat steps 2 and 3 for other objects in your artwork that you want to move to a separate layer.

Move Unselected Objects to a New Layer

You can restack objects without selecting them by moving layer listings on the Layers panel. Do one of the following:

■   Drag a <Path> layer listing onto one of the new top-level layer listings. Command-click (Mac OS) or Ctrl-click (Windows) several <Path> listings to drag multiple listings together (**Figure 5.30**).

TIP

To quickly select all of the nested objects within a top-level layer, click the blank area to the right of that top-level layer listing. All of the nested listings, and their related artboard objects, will be selected.

Figure 5.30 Moving the listing in the Layers panel

■   Click the blank area to the right of a <Path> listing to select that object. (It will also be selected in the document window.) Then drag the selection square onto a new top-level layer.

Restack Objects within a Layer

After you reorganize pieces of your artwork into individual layers, you may need to restack the objects within those layers.

1   On the Layers panel, expand one of the top-level layer listings.

2 Drag one of the nested <Path> listings above or below the other listings within that layer. Notice how this affects the stacking order of objects in your artwork (**Figures 5.31** and **5.32**).

LOCATE AN OBJECT LISTING QUICKLY ON THE LAYERS PANEL

When dozens of objects are nested within one layer, you may find it difficult to locate the listing for a specific object. To quickly locate an object listing in the Layers panel, select the object in the document window and then click the Locate Object button ⌕ at the bottom of the Layers panel. The top-level layer that contains the selected object automatically expands and the nested listing for that object is highlighted.

Figure 5.31 The Layers panel shows some of the hair objects stacked above the head listing. (Hair objects placed on top of the head were temporarily hidden for clarity.)

Figure 5.32 Drag the head listing upward to change its position in the stack and in the artwork.

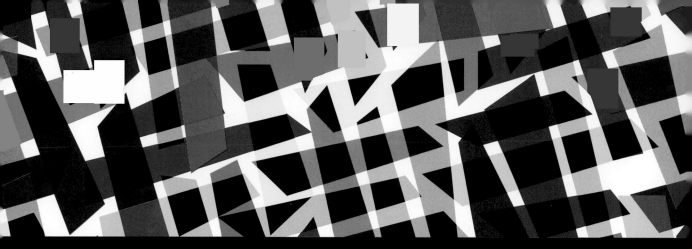

CHAPTER OBJECTIVES

Chapter Learning Objectives

- Align objects using guides.
- Draw an object from its center.
- Use the Shape Builder tool.
- Stack an object behind existing objects.

Chapter ACA Objectives

DOMAIN 3.0
UNDERSTANDING ADOBE ILLUSTRATOR CC

3.2 Define the functions of commonly used tools, including selection tools, the Pen tool, and other drawing tools, shape tools, and transformation tools.

3.4 Use non-printing design tools in the interface, such as rulers, guides, bleeds, and artboards.

DOMAIN 4.0
CREATING DIGITAL GRAPHICS AND ILLUSTRATIONS USING ADOBE ILLUSTRATOR CC

4.2 Use Vector drawing and shape tools.

4.4 Create and manage layers.

CHAPTER 6

Create a Logo

In this chapter, you will learn how to create a yin and yang symbol to use as a logo. The techniques you will acquire involve using guides and alignment commands for the perfect placement of drawn objects and uniting parts from simple shapes to create a more complex object.

▶ *Video Project 01-08* *Yin Yang Logo*

Precise Alignment of Objects

Illustrator provides nonprinting ruler guides and smart guides (both of which will not appear on paper or digital output) to help you position and align objects in your artwork.

★ *ACA Objective 3.4*

A Primer on Guides

Here's some key information on the guides available in Illustrator.

RULER GUIDES

First, you will need to display rulers along the top and left sides of the document window. To do this, choose View > Rulers > Show Rulers. Simply drag from either ruler into the document to place a ruler guide (**Figure 6.1**).

NOTE

This chapter supports the project created in Video Project 01. Go to the Video Project 01 page in the book's Web Edition to watch the entire project from beginning to end.

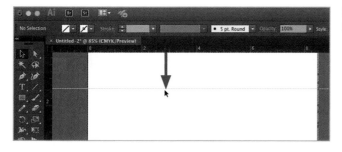

Figure 6.1 Dragging to place a ruler guide

Guides are useful as alignment aids when positioning objects in your artwork. When the View > Snap to Point feature is enabled (which it is by default), dragging any path edge, anchor point, or center point near a guide will cause that edge or point to snap to the guide.

NOTE *By default, a ruler guide will span from one edge of the document window to the other and across multiple artboards. When you want to limit a guide to a single artboard, select the Artboard tool, click to select an artboard, and then drag to create a ruler guide.*

To clear all guides (locked or unlocked), choose View > Guides > Clear Guides.

Ruler guides remain visible onscreen until you opt to hide them. You can lock them, making them nonselectable and unable to be moved purposefully or accidentally. And you can unlock them, making them selectable and able to be repositioned at any time. To delete an unlocked guide, select it using a selection tool, then press Delete (Mac OS) or Backspace (Windows). In the View > Guides submenu, you'll find options for locking and hiding guides.

Ruler guides are listed on the Layers panel as <Guide> as shown in **Figure 6.2**.

You can move a <Guide> listing onto its own layer, if you prefer. To show or hide a guide, click in the first column at left on the Layers panel to toggle the visibility icon. To lock or unlock guides, click in the second column at left to toggle the lock icon.

Figure 6.2 Ruler guides listed on the Layers panel

SMART GUIDES

Smart guides produce nonprinting labels and lines that temporarily appear onscreen when you drag to create, transform, or move an object. You can use them to quickly align an object with nearby edges, points, or center points of other objects. Smart guides also appear when you create, resize, or reposition artboards in Artboard mode.

When you roll over a selected or unselected object, smart guides will highlight its entire path and display labels such as "path," "anchor," or "center" to designate where those elements are located. Measurement labels also appear when you roll over an anchor point or draw an object.

You may choose View > Smart Guides, or press Command+U (Mac OS) or Ctrl+U (Windows) to turn this feature on and off.

Align Two Circles with Precision

To draw the first part of the logo:

1 Shift-drag with the Ellipse tool to draw a large circle. Apply a fill color, and leave the circle selected.

2 If necessary, press Command+R (Mac OS) or Ctrl+R (Windows) to display the rulers.

3 Choose View > Smart Guides to enable Smart Guides.

4 To help align the parts of the logo, drag a horizontal and vertical ruler guide and align each to the center point of the selected circle (**Figure 6.3**).

5 Double-click the Scale tool to select it and open the Scale dialog box. Or, choose Object > Transform > Scale.

6 In the Scale dialog box, enter **50** in the Uniform field, and click Copy.

7 Apply a different fill color to the copy.

8 Select both circles. On the Control or Align panel, click the Vertical Align Top button ▥ (**Figure 6.4**).

The smaller circle will be properly aligned with the top edge of the larger circle (**Figure 6.5**).

9 Click the artboard to deselect all objects.

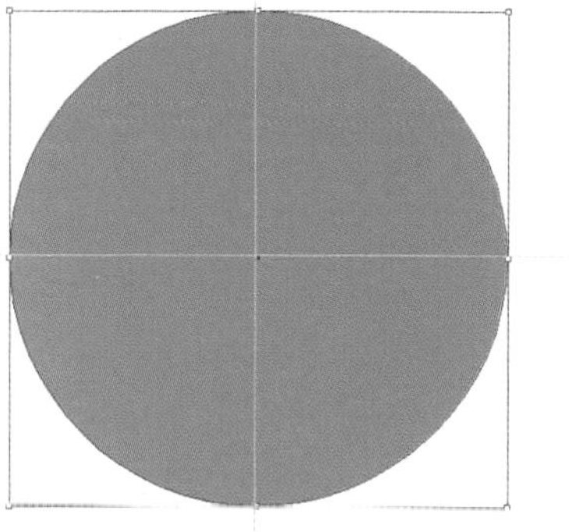

Figure 6.3 Guides on the circle

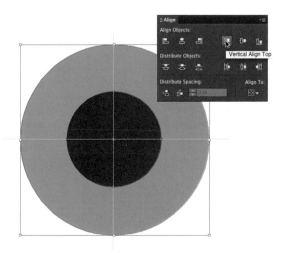

Figure 6.4 The Align panel and the selected circles

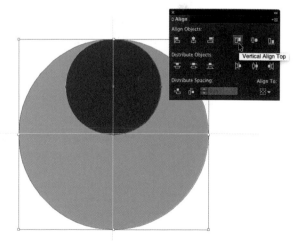

Figure 6.5 Circles aligned

Create a Second Small Circle

You'll need a second small circle to create the logo.

1 With the Selection tool, Option-drag (Mac OS) or Alt-drag (Windows) the upper small circle downward to create a copy.

2 To precisely align the copy vertically, drag downward along the vertical ruler guide or Shift-drag to constrain the drag to the vertical axis (**Figure 6.6**).

3 Shift-click to select both the large circle and the copy of the smaller circle. On the Control or Align panel, click the Vertical Align Bottom button (**Figure 6.7**).

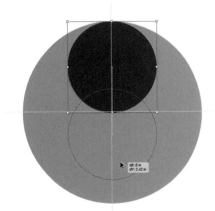

Figure 6.6 Dragging constrained to the vertical axis

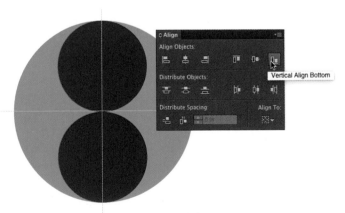

Figure 6.7 Vertically aligning the circle bottom

Create Two Smaller Circles

The final pieces you need for your logo are two smaller circles. You will use the smart guides labels to help align these new circles.

1 Zoom in and select the upper small circle.

2 Select the Ellipse tool. Position the pointer on the center point of the upper small circle to properly align the existing circle with the circle you're about to draw. The "center" label will appear.

3 Option-Shift-drag (Mac OS) or Alt-Shift-drag (Windows) to draw a circle from its center (**Figure 6.8**). Apply a fill color.

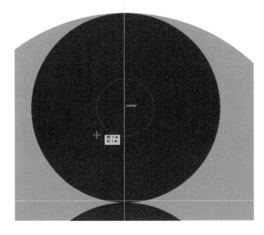

Figure 6.8 Drawing a circle from its center

4 Option-drag (Mac OS) or Alt-drag (Windows) the new circle downward along the vertical guide (or hold down Shift with the Option or Alt key to constrain the drawing). Stop when the "intersect" label appears.

The second new circle is now positioned over and intersecting the center point of the bottom circle.

Use the Shape Builder Tool

Now you're ready to unite parts of the largest circle with each of the smaller circles. In the process, you will convert the circle objects into the yin and yang shapes.

★ *ACA Objective 4.2*

Unite Portions of Separate Objects

Rather than cut up or divide objects and then combine the pieces to create a new shape, Illustrator provides the handy Shape Builder tool ⊕. To unite partially overlapping objects, you only need to drag the tool across areas where the objects intersect. A gray highlight texture temporarily appears over areas as you roll or drag across them and a temporary red border previews the united shape as you drag.

1   Select the large circle and both of the smaller circles.

2   Select the Shape Builder tool (or press Shift+M), and drag from the left area on the large circle across a smaller circle (**Figure 6.9**). A new, closed object shape is created.

3   Now drag from the other area of the large circle across the other smaller circle to create another closed object shape.

4   If necessary, change the fill color of the new shapes (**Figure 6.10**).

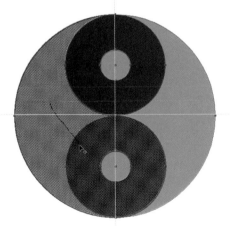

Figure 6.9 Dragging with the Shape Builder tool

Figure 6.10 The yin yang shape final shape build

Remove Areas Using the Shape Builder Tool

In addition to uniting parts of different objects, the Shape Builder tool can also remove parts of overlapping objects.

1   Option-click (Mac OS) or Alt-click (Windows) an overlapping area to exclude it (create a cutout) (**Figure 6.11**).

2 The resulting shape is listed as a compound object on the Layers panel. You can drag the corner points and edges of the cutout to modify its size.

3 Option-click (Mac OS) or Alt-click (Windows) a non-overlapping area to delete it from the resulting shape (**Figure 6.12**).

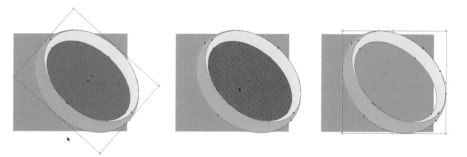

Figure 6.11 Creating a cutout in a combined shape

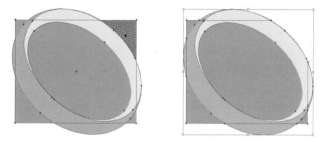

Figure 6.12 The side area removed

Shape Builder Tool Options

You can control settings and behaviors for the Shape Builder tool via its tool options dialog box.

1 Double-click the Shape Builder tool to open the Shape Builder Tool Options dialog box (**Figure 6.13**).

2 Select Gap Detection and select a size from the Gap Length menu to allow the tool to detect small gaps between selected objects (treating the areas on either side of the gap as separate areas).

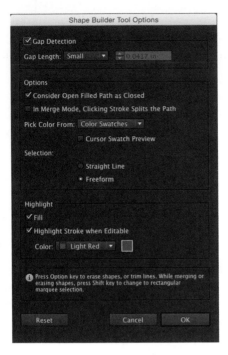

Shape Builder Tool Options

☑ Gap Detection

Gap Length: Small ▼ ⇕ 0.0417 in.

Options
✓ Consider Open Filled Path as Closed
☐ In Merge Mode, Clicking Stroke Splits the Path
Pick Color From: Color Swatches ▼
        ☐ Cursor Swatch Preview

Selection:
        ○ Straight Line
        ● Freeform

Highlight
✓ Fill
✓ Highlight Stroke when Editable
Color: ☐ Light Red ▼ ☐

ⓘ Press Option key to erase shapes, or trim lines. While merging or
erasing shapes, press Shift key to change to rectangular
marquee selection.

Reset   Cancel   OK

Figure 6.13 The Shape Builder Tool Options dialog box

3   From the Pick Color From menu, select Color Swatches to apply the most recently chosen swatch on the Swatches panel, or select Artwork to apply the fill color from the most recent area you dragged over.

4   Under Selection, choose Freeform to enable non-straight dragging of the tool when combining shape areas.

5   Click OK.

Stack an Object Behind

★ *ACA Objective 4.4*   You have one final element to add to the logo.

Create a Border Around the Circular Logo

The key steps to creating a larger circle around the logo are first to draw the circle from the center of the logo. Then, using the Layers panel, stack the new object below all of the other objects in the logo.

1 Using the Ellipse tool, position its pointer over the intersection of the horizontal and vertical ruler guides.

2 Option-Shift-drag (Mac OS) or Alt-Shift-drag (Windows) to draw a large circle from its center (**Figure 6.14**).

3 Apply a black fill color and set the stroke to None.

4 On the Layers panel, expand the top-level layer listing, and drag the nested <Path> listing (or its selection square) for the new circle below all of the other nested object listings on that layer (**Figure 6.15**).

5 When you are done creating your logo, choose View > Guides > Hide to hide all of the guides.

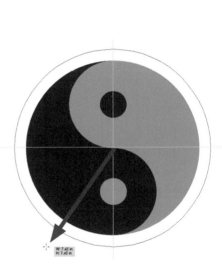

Figure 6.14 Drawing a large circle from its center

Figure 6.15 Restacking the black circle in the yin yang shape

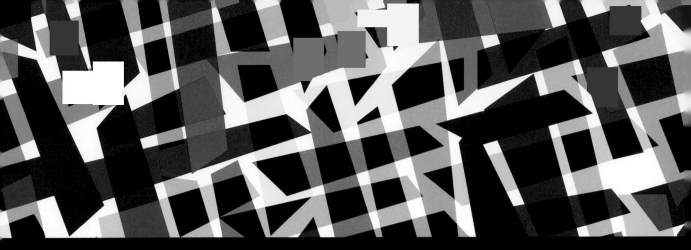

CHAPTER OBJECTIVES

Chapter Learning Objectives

- Reshape objects via transformations.
- Combine objects via Pathfinder options.
- Apply effects to objects.
- Edit effects.
- Save effects as a graphic style.

Chapter ACA Objectives

DOMAIN 4.0
CREATING DIGITAL GRAPHICS AND
ILLUSTRATIONS USING ADOBE ILLUSTRATOR CC

4.2   Use vector drawing and shape tools.

4.3   Transform graphics and illustrations.

CHAPTER 7

Complexity via Combination and Effects

In this chapter, you will use transformations, commands, and effects to produce even more complex shapes. You will first learn how you can modify basic shapes by applying a set of Pathfinder commands that unite or divide objects—rather than by manually altering segments and points as you learned earlier. Then you will apply effects to perform modifications that remain "live" (editable) even after they've been applied.

Reshape via Transformation

When creating more complex shapes, you can use transformations to reshape the points and segments on an object. In the next task, you will learn how to use two transform methods to move two points on a path inward symmetrically to taper the side of an object.

NOTE

This chapter supports the project created in Video Project 02. Go to the Video Project 02 page in the book's Web Edition to watch the entire project from beginning to end.

★ *ACA Objective 4.3*

▶ *Video Project 02-01 Gears*

Understand the Scale tool vs. the Free Transform Tool

You can reshape a path using the transform options of the Scale tool or Free Transform tool.

To use the Scale tool:

1 Shift-click to select two anchor points.

2 Select the Scale tool (or press S).

3 Drag inward or outward to symmetrically reposition both points.

   Because you selected two points, only the distance between those points can be "scaled" or altered (**Figure 7.1**).

Figure 7.1 Repositioning anchor points via Scale tool

To use the Free Transform tool:

1 Select an object.

2 Select the Free Transform tool (or press E).

   A bounding box appears around the object along with a movable widget with four icons.

3 The Free Transform (second) icon is selected automatically so you can scale the object by dragging out a corner handle, rotate it by dragging a corner handle clockwise or counterclockwise, and shear it by dragging a side handle.

4 Click the Perspective (third) icon down, and drag a corner handle inward or outward (**Figure 7.2**).

   TIP *Click the Constrain (top) icon on the widget to limit changes to the following transformations: scale proportionally, rotate at 45° increments, or shear along the horizontal or vertical axis.*

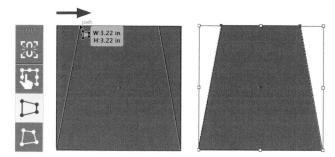

Figure 7.2 Adjusting perspective via Free Transform tool

Combine via Pathfinder Options

When creating a more complex shape, instead of using a drawing tool to draw every bend and turn of a path, you can take an easier approach and combine objects to create the desired contour of the overall shape.

The Pathfinder panel (Window > Pathfinder) contains the options to combine or divide overlapping objects. The options on the panel are organized into two groups: Shape Mode options and Pathfinder options.

The upper portion of the Pathfinder panel contains Shape Mode icons for the Unite, Minus Front, Intersect, and Exclude options (**Figure 7.3**). Each option combines overlapping objects in a unique way.

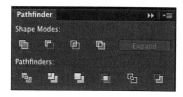

Figure 7.3 The Pathfinder panel

Shape Modes: Two Different Results

The Shape Modes options can produce either a path or a compound shape, depending on whether you just click an icon to create a path, or Option-click (Mac OS) or Alt-click (Windows) an icon to create a compound shape.

UNITE AS AN OBJECT

You can use Unite to join the edges of multiple selected, overlapping objects into a single object. The attributes of the frontmost object are applied to the resulting object.

Assemble some objects into an overlapping shape and select all the objects (**Figure 7.4**). On the Pathfinder panel, click the Unite icon to create a single path object (**Figure 7.5**).

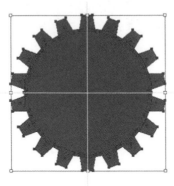

Figure 7.4 Select all the objects.   **Figure 7.5** Create a single path object.

UNITE AS A COMPOUND SHAPE

When you Option-click (Mac OS) or Alt-click (Windows) the Unite icon, a **compound shape** (rather than a single path) is created. The original objects in compound shapes are preserved. On the Layers panel, you can expand the Compound Shape listing to view the listings for the nested, preserved objects.

Compound shapes provide greater editing flexibility. You can select an individual object within the united shape and move, reshape, or hide it to alter the contour of the overall compound shape at any time. To try this:

1   Assemble some objects into an overlapping shape. Select all the objects.

2   Option-click (Mac OS) or Alt-click (Windows) the Unite icon on the Pathfinder panel (**Figure 7.6**).

3   Press Command+U (Mac OS) or Ctrl+U (Windows) to enable smart guides.

4   Position the pointer over the united object to display the paths of nested objects. Using the Direct Selection tool, select nested objects and reposition or reshape them. Press V to display and access an object's bounding box (**Figure 7.7**).

Figure 7.6 The resulting compound shape

Figure 7.7 The shape with the nested objects reshaped

EXPAND

You can click the Expand button on the Pathfinder panel to convert any selected compound shape into a single path (for objects created using Unite and Intersect) or a compound path (for objects created using Exclude, discussed later).

MINUS FRONT

Use Minus Front when you want to cut away selected objects from the underlying backmost object. The attributes of the backmost object are applied to the resulting object. The overlapping objects are not saved.

Place smaller objects in front of a larger object (**Figure 7.8**). Select all of the objects. On the Pathfinder panel, click the Minus Front icon 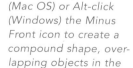.

The frontmost objects will create holes in the larger back object (**Figure 7.9**).

TIP

When you Option-click (Mac OS) or Alt-click (Windows) the Minus Front icon to create a compound shape, overlapping objects in the shape are preserved and hidden.

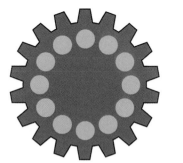

Figure 7.8 Smaller objects placed in front of the larger object

Figure 7.9 Holes created in the back object by the subtraction of the frontmost objects

Figure 7.10 Drag the path to reposition the cutout.

Figure 7.11 Two selected objects (left), intersect results (center), copy of original oval placed behind intersect results

NOTE *To demonstrate the editing flexibility of vector objects, with the Direct Selection tool, Option-click (Mac OS) or Alt-click (Windows) the edge of any cutout area. Drag the path to reposition the cutout (**Figure 7.10**). (Amazing, yes!)*

INTERSECT

Use Intersect to preserve only the area in which all the objects overlap. All non-overlapping areas are hidden. The attributes of the frontmost object are applied to the resulting object (**Figure 7.11**).

EXCLUDE

Use Exclude to preserve only the areas where all of the objects do *not* overlap. All overlapping areas become cutouts.

Assemble some objects into an overlapping shape. Select all the objects (**Figure 7.12**). On the Pathfinder panel, click the Exclude icon. Any overlapping areas become cutouts (**Figure 7.13**).

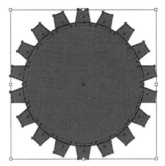

Figure 7.12 Exclude selection

Figure 7.13 Exclude result

Pathfinder Options

The lower area of the Pathfinder panel contains a row of icons that also break up overlapping objects into separate, non-overlapping, closed paths nested within a group. The original objects are not preserved. Let's explore one of the Pathfinder options, Divide.

DIVIDE

Use the Divide command to convert overlapping areas into separate, non-overlapping objects.

1   Select two or more partially overlapping objects.

2   On the Pathfinder panel, click the Divide icon . Overlapping areas convert into separate, flat objects.

3   Press A to select the Direct Selection tool. Click each of the divided objects, and apply individual color fills to each one to create an elaborate pattern of colors (**Figure 7.14**).

TIP
A separate, flat object can also be deleted or given a fill of None to create a cutout in the pattern.

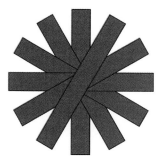 

Figure 7.14 The original objects (left) and the Divide results (right). Color was applied to the fill of some of the divided objects.

Apply Effects to an Object

You can apply effects, such as distortion and stylistic changes, to an object to produce results that range from subtle to pronounced. Effects are applied using the Appearance panel or the Effect menu.

★ *ACA Objective 4.2*

Effects change only the appearance of an object and not its underlying path. You can edit or delete effects at any time without permanently altering the object to

which they are applied. You also can apply multiple effects to an object and those effects can remain independent of each other. That is, a change to one effect will not alter any other effects. Better still, effects are live. If you reshape the path of the underlying object, the effects will adjust accordingly.

1 Select an object, and do one of the following:

- From the Effect menu, select an Illustrator effect from the categories listed at the top.

- At the bottom of the Appearance panel, from the Add New Effect menu, select an Illustrator effect from the categories listed at the top (**Figure 7.15**).

2 In the effect's dialog box, select Preview.

3 Modify any settings or options you want. Press Tab to update the preview (**Figure 7.16**).

4 Click OK. The effect is applied to the object and listed on the Appearance panel.

Figure 7.15 The Add New Effect menu on the Appearance panel

TIP *By default, an effect is applied to an entire object. If you drag the effect listing on the Appearance panel over the Stroke or Fill listing and release the mouse button, the effect will be nested within that listing and modify only that attribute. Drag the effect listing out of the expanded Stroke or Fill listing to once again apply it to the entire object.*

Figure 7.16 Applying different effects to an object

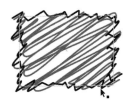 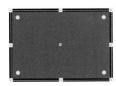 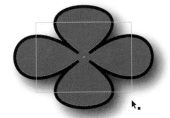

Edit an Effect

TIP

To remove an effect, on the Appearance panel, click next to the effect's name to highlight its listing. Then, click the Delete Selected Item icon at the bottom of the Appearance panel.

You can edit or remove effects at any time.

1 Select an object that contains an effect.

2 On the Appearance panel, click the underlined effect name. (If you nested the effect within the Stroke or Fill attribute, expand that listing to access the effect link.)

3 In the dialog box that opens, adjust any settings or options, and click OK.

Save Effects as Styles

On the Graphic Styles panel, you can save the current settings for an applied effect as a style for repeated use. Effect settings saved as styles can be quickly applied to other objects with one click.

1   Select an object that contains one or more effects.

2   Choose Window > Graphic Styles to open the Graphic Styles panel. At the bottom of the panel, click the New Graphic Style icon.

The current Stroke, Fill, and effects settings of the selected object are saved as a style, and a new thumbnail appears on the Graphic Styles panel as the last thumbnail.

3   Double-click the thumbnail, enter a name for the style, and click OK to accept the new filename.

4   To apply the saved style to another object, select that object. On the Graphic Styles panel, click the graphic style's thumbnail.

TIP *When a graphic style is applied to a selected object, the style name is listed at the top of the Appearance panel. To remove a graphic style from a selected object, from the Appearance panel menu, select Reduce to Basic Appearance.*

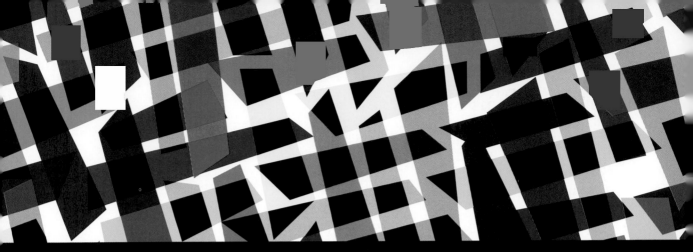

CHAPTER OBJECTIVES

Chapter Learning Objectives

- Create spiraling imagery.
- Apply distortion via tools.
- Apply variable stroke widths to line work.
- Group objects for better organization.
- Use selection commands.

Chapter ACA Objectives

DOMAIN 3.0
UNDERSTANDING ADOBE ILLUSTRATOR CC

3.8 Demonstrate knowledge of how and why illustrators employ different views and modes throughout the course of a project, including vector/appearance, isolation mode, and various Draw modes.

DOMAIN 4.0
CREATING DIGITAL GRAPHICS AND ILLUSTRATIONS USING ADOBE ILLUSTRATOR CC

4.3 Transform graphics and illustrations.

4.4 Create and manage layers.

CHAPTER 8

Hand-drawn Look Applied to Shapes

In this chapter, you will learn how to use repetition to create spiral designs that are composed of multiple elements. You'll learn about the warp tools that apply hand-drawn distortion to objects, about a width tool that applies different stroke thickness to a line, and about quick, efficient ways to select specific elements in a complex design. You will also learn how to group objects together to help organize the many elements that now make up your artwork.

NOTE

This chapter supports the project created in Video Project 02. Go to the Video Project 02 page in the book's Web Edition to watch the entire project from beginning to end.

Create Spirals

The Spiral tool is used to create spiral shapes. You can modify certain components of the spiral while you are creating it.

▶ *Video Project 02-02* Creating *Spirals*

1 Select the Spiral tool 🌀 on the Tools panel.

2 Drag across an artboard from where you want the center of the spiral to be.

3 While dragging, do any of the following (**Figure 8.1**):

   ■ To scale the spiral, drag away from or toward the center.

   ■ To control how tightly the spirals wind toward the center, Command-drag (Mac OS) or Ctrl-drag (Windows) away from or toward the center.

   ■ To add or delete segments in the center of the spiral, press the Up Arrow or Down Arrow key.

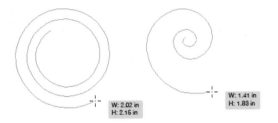

Figure 8.1 A tight spiral (left) and a loose spiral (right) created with the Spiral tool

Figure 8.2 A completed spiral object with the current fill and stroke settings applied

4   Release the mouse button to complete the spiral.

The new spiral is selected and the current fill and stroke settings are applied to it (**Figure 8.2**).

Distortion Tools

★ *ACA Objective 4.3*

Figure 8.3 The seven Liquify tools

The seven Liquify tools (also referred to as the Warp tools) apply distortion to objects by moving the anchor points and handles on the path in random, non-uniform directions. You can use these tools to lend a rough, hand-drawn look to vector objects composed of smooth, uniform edges. Of the seven tools, you'll use Warp, Twirl, Pucker, and Bloat more frequently because they make it easier to control the applied distortion.

1   On the Tools panel, click the Width tool icon 🖉 and select a Liquify tool from the menu of hidden tools (**Figure 8.3**).

2   Click or drag along the path of an unselected or selected object.

Figures 8.4 and **8.5** show shape distortions you can create with these tools.

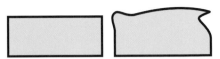

Figure 8.4 The original object (left), Warp tool edit (right)

Figure 8.5 Pucker tool edit (left), Bloat tool edit (right)

Each of the seven Liquify tools provides a set of options for customizing the behavior of the tool. Double-click a Liquify tool icon to open its Tool Options dialog box (**Figure 8.6**).

Changes made to the Global Brush Dimensions options will be applied to all the Liquify tools. The Intensity option determines the amount of distortion applied to a path. Keep this option at a low value to apply less distortion and gain more control when using the tool.

Options in the middle of the dialog box are based on, and apply to, the currently selected tool only.

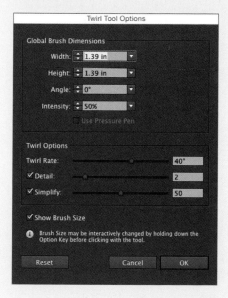

Figure 8.6 The Twirl Tool Options dialog box

Variable Line Widths

Vector drawing tools create lines of uniform width. Using the Width tool, you can apply variable widths (thicknesses) to your line work to make it appear more like lines created with a traditional pen or pencil.

Apply a Width Preset

You can initially learn about applying variable widths to paths by working with predefined width profiles.

TIP

The Variable Width Profile menu is also accessible (as the Profile menu) at the bottom of the fully expanded Stroke panel.

1. Select an open path line or a closed path shape.

2. Apply a stroke between 8 and 10 points to the object to better visualize the next steps (**Figure 8.7**).

3. On the Control panel, from the Variable Width Profile menu, select a predefined width profile to apply it to the selected object (**Figure 8.8**). Increase the stroke width to increase the variable width effect.

4. Optional: From the Variable Width Profile menu, select Uniform to remove any variable width produced via a profile or the Width tool.

Figure 8.7 An object with a uniform stroke

Figure 8.8 Choosing a Width Profile (left); the Width Profile applied (right)

Reshape a Stroke Manually

Now that you've seen examples of variable widths on a path, it's time to create your own custom width line work.

TIP

Using the Width tool, you can roll over an object to highlight a width point and its handles. Option-drag (Mac OS) or Alt-drag (Windows) a width handle to modify one side of the variable width only.

1. Select the Width tool (Shift+W). Zoom in on an unselected object.

2. Roll over the path of the object. Click and drag outward to place a diamond shape width point and widen the stroke.

   The point displays a pair of handles whose lengths determine the custom width (**Figure 8.9**).

Figure 8.9 Widening the stroke

3. Drag to reposition the point, if desired. Option-drag (Mac OS) or Alt-drag (Windows) to create a copy of the width point. If you need to remove a selected point, press Delete (Mac OS) or Backspace (Windows).

4. Click and drag inward from the edge of the stroke to place a diamond shape width point and narrow the stroke (**Figure 8.10**). Drag to reposition the point, if desired.

Figure 8.10 Narrowing the stroke

Create a Custom Width Profile Preset

After creating a custom width shape you like, you can save it for repeated use.

1. Alter the stroke width on an object's path. Keep the object selected.

2. On the Control panel, at the bottom of the menu, click the Add To Profiles icon. In the Variable Width Profile dialog box that appears, enter a name for the profile, then click OK.

3. Your new custom profile appears at the bottom of the menu and can be applied as a profile to the stroke of any selected object (**Figure 8.11**).

> **TIP** *To delete a custom profile, deselect all, then click the profile on the Variable Width Profile menu to select it. Click the menu again to reopen it, then click the Delete Profile button at the bottom of the menu. Click Yes in the alert.*

Figure 8.11 Creating a custom profile

Group Objects

★ ACA Objective 4.4

Use the Group command to create a collection of objects that make up an element in your design. Grouping objects together produces better organization both in your artwork and on the Layers panel (**Figure 8.12**). As you have seen in the complex design of the rotated spirals, collecting the spiral object, twirled square, and small circles into a group makes it easier to select, scale, and reposition those elements as a single entity.

1 In your artwork, select two or more objects that are being used to create an element or shape.

2 To group the objects together, press Command+G (Mac OS) or Ctrl+G (Windows). You can also choose Object > Group. Click the artboard to deselect all objects.

> **TIP** To ungroup a selected group, press Command+Shift+G (Mac OS) or Ctrl+Shift+G (Windows), or choose Object > Ungroup.

3 Click any part of the group.

All the objects become selected and a bounding box displays around the entire group.

4 When working with a group, you can:

- Reposition the selected group by dragging any object in the group.
- Apply a transformation to the group via its bounding box, the Object menu commands, or the transform tools.

Figure 8.12 A selected group (left); a selected group listed on the Layers panel (right)

Isolate a Group

When you double-click a group in your artwork, the grouped objects are placed in isolation mode, enabling you to edit only those objects (**Figure** 8.13).

★ *ACA Objective 3.8*

1   Using the Selection tool ▶, double-click a group.

   ▪ Objects within the group are shown in full color and are editable.

   ▪ Objects outside the group are temporarily dimmed and uneditable.

   ▪ A gray isolation mode bar appears across the top of the document window.

   ▪ The current layer and group names are listed in the bar.

2   Use the Selection tool to select and edit an isolated object. Use the Direct Selection tool to select and edit a point or segment on an isolated object.

3   To exit isolation mode, click the gray isolation mode bar, press Esc, or double-click a blank area of an artboard.

Figure 8.13 Isolation mode

Selection Commands

As your designs become a complex assembly of many objects, you may find it more difficult to quickly select just one type of object in the design and edit those objects. Wouldn't it be great if there were a way to select specific types of objects? Well, there is. The Select menu provides commands for selecting objects that share a specific attribute.

1   Select an object that contains an attribute you want to edit throughout the design.

2   From the Select > Same submenu (**Figure 8.14**), select an option to search for that attribute. The command will search through every object in the document.

   Any objects that contain the same attribute are selected.

3   Edit the attribute, then deselect.

Figure 8.14 The Select > Same menu

Select Same Options

Following is a brief explanation of what some of the Select > Same options will search for:

- Fill Color, Opacity, Stroke Color, and Stroke Weight are straightforward commands that search for one attribute only.

- Appearance will search for objects that contain all the appearances currently listed on the Appearance panel of the selected object.

- Appearance Attribute will search for the specific attribute listing that is currently highlighted on the Appearance panel for the selected object.

- Graphic Style will search for the currently selected thumbnail on the Graphic Styles panel. The name of the selected graphic style will also be listed at the top of the Appearance panel.

Select Similar Options

The Control panel offers its own menu for accessing selection options along with a quick-click method for applying the currently selected options.

1. On the Control panel, click the Select Similar Options menu to display a list of most of the commands found on the Select > Same submenu (**Figure 8.15**).

2. Select an option to make it the current attribute to search for.

Figure 8.15 The Select Similar Options menu on the Control panel

3. Any objects that contain the searched for attribute will become selected.

Scale Options for Strokes

Before scaling an object or a group of objects, you can decide whether any applied strokes and effects should also be scaled using the Scale Strokes & Effects option.

You can find this option in the following places in Illustrator:

- At the bottom of the Transform panel.
- At the bottom of the Scale dialog box. To open the Scale dialog box, double-click the Scale tool .
- From the Object > Transform > Scale dialog box.
- In the Preferences > General panel.

TIP

Toggling Scale Strokes & Effects in one location automatically enables or disables that setting in all the other locations.

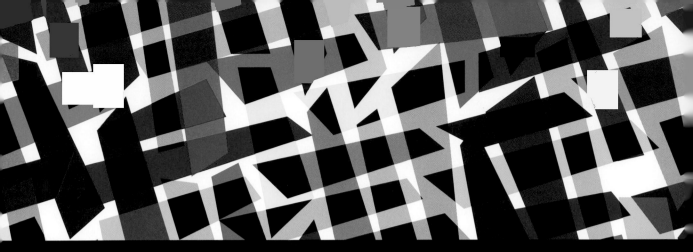

CHAPTER OBJECTIVES

Chapter Learning Objectives

- Create a Live Paint group.
- Use the Live Paint Bucket tool.
- Add new paths to a Live Paint group.
- Apply color to the edges of a Live Paint group.
- Expand or release a Live Paint group.

Chapter ACA Objectives

DOMAIN 4.0
CREATING DIGITAL GRAPHICS AND
ILLUSTRATIONS USING ADOBE ILLUSTRATOR CC

4.3 Transform graphics and illustrations.

CHAPTER 9

Live Paint

In this chapter, you will work with Live Paint, a feature that provides a novel way to fill paths. In fact, the paths don't even have to be closed paths. You can use the drawing tools to create intersecting lines, and convert your line work into a Live Paint group.

Then, you can use the Live Paint Bucket to apply a color by clicking or by dragging across an area formed by the intersecting lines (called a face) to apply color. Reposition or reshape any of the drawing lines and the fill color flows into the new shape. This is the "live" aspect of the feature. With Live Paint, you can even apply strokes to segments of a line—something you can't do with a standard Illustrator object.

NOTE

This chapter supports the project created in Video Project 01. Go to the Video Project 01 page in the book's Web Edition to watch the entire project from beginning to end.

Create a Live Paint Group

★ *ACA Objective 4.3*

▶ *Video Project 01-06 Introduction to Live Paint*

To start working with Live Paint, you first need to create some intersecting lines using the Pencil, Pen, or Line Segment tool. The lines need to intersect because the Live Paint Bucket tool, which you'll use to color areas, needs to detect that an area is closed (that is, no gaps occur where lines intersect). Don't bother applying any complex appearances to the lines (such as brushes, transparency, and variable stroke widths) because, as an alert will warn you, those attributes are lost when converting to a Live Paint group.

1   Using the Pencil tool ✐, draw some intersecting lines. Apply a stroke of 1 or 2 pts (**Figure 9.1**).

2   Select all of the path objects, and then do one of the following:

- Select the Live Paint Bucket tool 🪣 (K), and click inside the selection.
- Choose Object > Live Paint > Make.

A Live Paint group is created and a red highlight appears along the border of the enclosed area that is under the pointer (**Figure 9.2**).

You will fill these areas, after you learn about gap options in Live Paint.

Figure 9.1 A line art robot created with the Pencil tool

Figure 9.2 The Live Paint Bucket tool highlights an enclosed area underneath it. The Cursor Swatch Preview displays above the bucket icon pointer.

Use Gap Options in a Live Paint Group

If you click with the Live Paint Bucket tool on a selection of intersecting lines and nothing happens, you may have gaps where lines appear to intersect.

1   To fix this situation, choose View > Show Live Paint Gaps (if the option says Hide, it's already on). Then, do one of the following:

- If the gaps are large, select the Direct Selection tool ▷ and drag the end point of one line across another line to close the gap.
- If the gaps are small, select the Live Paint Bucket tool and click the Gap Options icon on the Control panel (next to the Expand button). Or, you can choose Object > Live Paint > Gap Options.

2   In the Gap Options dialog box (**Figure 9.3**), select Gap Detection and Preview.

3   Select an option from the Paint Stops At menu.

Short red line indicators will appear across any gaps in the line work, signifying that the Live Paint feature now considers those areas to be closed and able to be filled (**Figure 9.4**).

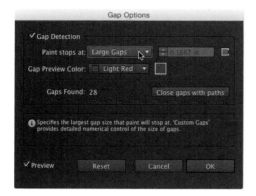

Figure 9.3 The Gap Options dialog box

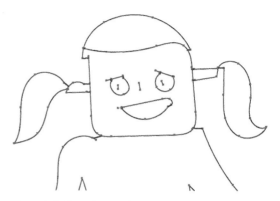

Figure 9.4 Gaps detected

Live Paint Bucket Tool

When you apply a fill color to a Live Paint group, faces (areas) take on that color rather than the actual paths. If you reshape your line work in any way, the fill color will reflow into the new shapes.

1   Select the Live Paint Bucket tool (or press K).

2   On the Swatches panel, click the Fill square. Click the swatch color you want to apply first.

This color will display above the pointer as the middle color in the Cursor Swatch Preview. You can select a solid color, pattern, or gradient swatch as the fill "color."

3   Roll the pointer over a face in the Live Paint group (no need to first select the group), and click to apply the color currently in the middle swatch preview (**Figure 9.5**).

TIP

Drag across multiple faces using the Live Paint Bucket tool to highlight those areas, and then click to apply the current fill color to all of those faces.

4 Roll the pointer over another face to highlight it. Press the Left or Right Arrow key to cycle through the previous or next swatch on the Swatches panel, and click to apply that color (**Figure 9.6**).

Figure 9.5 Filling in the shapes with the Paint Bucket tool

Figure 9.6 All fill colors applied

Add New Paths to a Live Paint Group

You can draw additional closed or open path objects, and then merge these objects into an existing Live Paint group.

1 Draw lines or a closed path object over an existing Live Paint group. Apply a stroke color of black and a fill of None (**Figure 9.7**).

2 Select both the new object and the Live Paint group. On the Control panel, click the Merge Live Paint button.

   The new object is now merged into the Live Paint group.

3 Choose the Live Paint Bucket tool and roll over any new faces that were created where existing lines intersect with lines in the merged object; this highlights them. Click to apply a color fill (**Figure 9.8**).

Figure 9.7 Additional lines were drawn to create background shapes around the robot.

Figure 9.8 The merged lines created new areas of intersection, and the Live Paint Bucket filled those faces with color. The merged lines also cross through the robot shape and extend off the edges of the artwork.

Edit Paths in a Live Paint Group

You can edit any path in a Live Paint group using the editing methods you've already learned.

To modify a single line, select a path with the Direct Selection tool, and drag to move anchor points or to reshape segments.

To modify lines or faces in the group:

1 Using the Selection tool, double-click a Live Paint group to enter isolation mode.

2 Click a colored face or a line to display its bounding box (**Figure 9.9**).

3 Drag to reposition the selection, or drag a handle to scale the selection.

4 Press Esc to exit isolation mode.

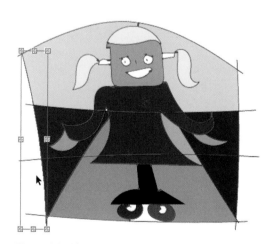

Figure 9.9 Object in group selected

> **TIP** *Beware: Your edits may produce new line intersections and cause surrounding colors to reflow into any newly created faces (areas). Moving a line may create gaps that will remove or reflow color fills.*

Apply Color to Edges

You can also use the Live Paint Bucket tool to apply separate stroke colors to each edge of a Live Paint group. An edge is any line segment that borders a face. Edge segments are created by the intersection of lines in the group.

TIP

Apply a stroke color of None to hide an edge. Use this technique to hide line segments that extend beyond any filled faces.

1   Double-click the Live Paint Bucket tool. In the Live Paint Bucket Options dialog box, under Options, select Paint Strokes. Click OK.

2   On the Swatches panel, select the Stroke square. Click the swatch color you want to apply to place it in the middle color preview for the tool.

3   Position the Live Paint Bucket tool over an edge segment. The pointer will change from a bucket icon to a brush icon and the highlight width will become thinner. Click an edge to change its color (**Figure 9.10**).

4   Roll over another segment, and press the Left Arrow and Right Arrow keys to switch the middle color preview choice.

5   On the Stroke panel, you can increase the Weight value to create a thicker stroke (**Figure 9.11**).

NOTE *You can modify the stroke width and stroke color for an entire Live Paint group. Select the group, change the Weight value on the Stroke panel, and apply a new stroke color. Doing so, however, will remove any custom stroke color and width selectively applied to the edges.*

Figure 9.10 New colors and stroke thicknesses were applied to some of the edges on the hair shapes with the Live Paint Bucket tool.

Figure 9.11 The image after applying colors to some of the edges and hiding the black line edges that cross through the robot and extend off the sides of the artwork

Expand or Release a Live Paint Group

You cannot apply appearance attributes (such as brush strokes, transparency, and effects) to the individual faces or edges of a Live Paint group. To apply these attributes, you need to expand or release the group into standard Illustrator objects. A Live Paint group also needs to be expanded or released before you can export your artwork file to a non-Adobe application.

1   Select a Live Paint group. Optionally, drag to create a copy of the group to preserve it for later use.

2   Do one of the following:

■   On the Control panel, click the Expand button to convert the separate paths in the Live Paint group into two nested groups of paths. One group will contain standard filled path objects made from the former faces. The other group will contain standard path objects with strokes (and no fill) from the former edges (**Figure 9.12**).

■   Choose Object > Live Paint> Release to convert the Live Paint group into separate path objects, each with a thin black stroke and a fill of None. The paths are contained within a group. Use this option when you want to convert your art back into line work, and then create a new Live Paint group and recolor the artwork using the Live Paint Bucket tool.

Figure 9.12 The Layers panel with Layer 10 expanded

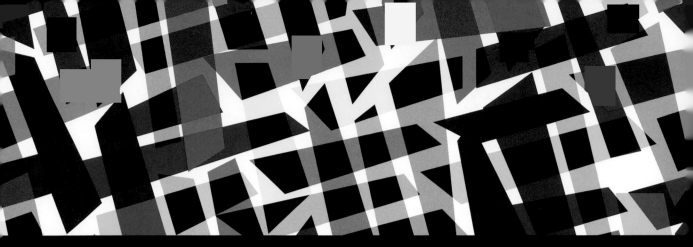

CHAPTER OBJECTIVES

Chapter Learning Objectives

- Draw shapes by cutting up larger shapes.
- Create a compound path.
- Add gradient fills to objects.
- Create and save custom gradients.
- Edit gradients via on-object controls.

Chapter ACA Objectives

DOMAIN 3.0
UNDERSTANDING ADOBE ILLUSTRATOR CC

3.6 Manage colors, swatches, and gradients.

CHAPTER 10

Cut Objects and Apply Gradients

In the earlier chapters, you explored how to create, reshape, and combine basic objects to create shapes. Illustrator also provides methods for "drawing" shapes using your own drawing skills. In this chapter, you will learn how to use the Knife tool to cut a larger object into more intricately shaped objects. You will also learn how to create, apply, and edit gradient fills to add more color variation to objects.

NOTE

This chapter supports the project created in Video Project 02. Go to the Video Project 02 page in the book's Web Edition to watch the entire project from beginning to end.

Draw Shapes by Cutting

The Knife tool in Illustrator enables you to draw freehand lines that will manually divide a larger object into separate, smaller shapes. As you drag the Knife tool across the larger shape, from one edge to the other, you create a path that follows the movement of the cursor. Illustrator automatically cuts the larger path and joins the two open segments to the newly drawn path. The result is two separate, closed objects.

▶ *Video Project 02-03 Knife Tool and Gradients*

1. Draw a large rectangle. Apply a stroke color and a fill color. Deselect the new object.

2. Select the Knife tool ✎, which is in the tool group with the Eraser tool ◢. Drag across the object, starting and ending outside the object's path either on the same side or across to another side.

   Illustrator creates two separate, closed objects with the stroke and fill attributes of the former large object.

3 Draw across the larger objects to create other more narrowly shaped objects (**Figure 10.1**).

Apply a separate fill color to some or all of the new objects (**Figure 10.2**).

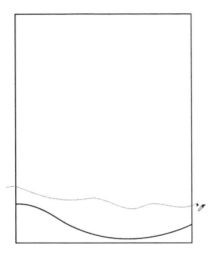

Figure 10.1 Drag the Knife tool across a larger object to create more narrow objects.

Figure 10.2 A landscape created by applying fills to objects created with the Knife tool

Create Compound Paths

A **compound path** is an object that contains within it a smaller, transparent subpath that creates a hole in the larger object. Compound paths provide editing flexibility: You can release the subpath from the larger object at any time.

You can create a compound path by placing one or more smaller objects in front of a larger object. To do this:

1 Place a smaller object in front of a larger object.

2 Select both objects, then do either of the following:

- Choose Object > Compound Path > Make.
- Control-click (Mac OS) or right-click (Windows) and choose Make Compound Path from the context menu (**Figure 10.3**).

The smaller object is combined with the larger object and becomes a transparent hole (**Figure 10.4**).

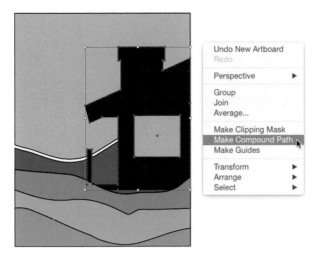

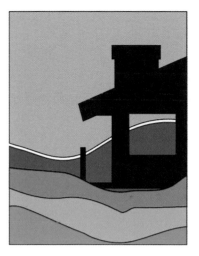

Figure 10.3 Creating a compound path from two objects

Figure 10.4 The smaller object creates a transparent hole in the larger object.

Release a Compound Path

You can release any subpaths by selecting the compound path object, then either choosing Object > Compound Path > Release or Control-clicking (Mac OS) or right-clicking (Windows) and selecting Release Compound Path from the context menu. Subpaths will become separate objects, stacked above the former compound path object, and all released objects will adopt the attributes of the former compound path.

If the compound path has a stroke of None, you can use the Smart Guides feature to locate the paths of the new objects.

Add Gradient Fills

★ *ACA Objective 3.6*

A **gradient fill** is a gradual blend between two or more solid colors. You can use gradients to add shading or volume in shapes to create the appearance of depth in flat objects.

A gradient fill is composed of a starting and ending color. You can place additional solid colors between the start and end colors for more color variation in the fill. The gradient can spread from side to side across an object (linear) or outward from the center of an object (radial).

To have some gradient swatches to work with, click the Swatch Libraries menu on the bottom of the Swatches panel and select a library from the Gradients submenu.

Apply a Gradient as a Fill

It's time to apply a gradient swatch to an object.

To apply a gradient fill:

1   To begin, select an object, then do either of the following:

- Display the Swatches panel, click the Fill square on the panel, then click a swatch on the panel or on any open gradient library panel to apply it.

- Display the full Gradient panel (click the double arrows on the panel tab, if necessary), then click the Fill square on the panel. Click the arrowhead next to the Gradient square to open the gradient menu, then select a gradient on the menu. Gradients on the main Swatches panel are listed on this menu (**Figure 10.5**).

Figure 10.5 Choosing and applying a gradient from the Gradient panel

Apply a Gradient to a Stroke

In addition to applying a gradient to an object's fill, you can apply a gradient along or across an object's stroke.

To apply a gradient to a stroke:

1   Select an object. Apply a large stroke weight to better view the gradient you are about to apply.

2   Do either of the following:

- Click the Stroke square on the main Gradient panel. Click the arrowhead next to the Gradient square to open the gradient menu, then select a gradient on the menu (**Figure 10.6**).

- Click the Stroke square on the Swatches panel, then click a gradient swatch on the panel or on any open gradient library panel to apply it.

By default, the gradient will display within the stroke from left to right, with no attempt to follow the shape of the stroke.

Figure 10.6 Applying a gradient to a stroke

3 To reorient the gradient to follow along or across the shape of the stroke, first make sure Align Stroke to Center is selected on the Stroke panel.

4 Next, on the Gradient panel, click the Stroke square. Click the Apply Gradient Along Stroke (**Figure 10.7**) or Apply Gradient Across Stroke icon (**Figure 10.8**).

Figure 10.7 Applying a gradient along a stroke

Figure 10.8 Applying a gradient across a stroke

Create a Custom Gradient

A custom gradient can be composed of all CMYK colors, all RGB process colors, or color tints of a spot color. You'll produce a custom gradient by first creating a two-color gradient.

To create a custom gradient:

1 Select an object. Display the full Gradient panel (click the double arrows on the panel tab, if necessary).

2 Click the Fill square. Double-click the left color stop below the gradient bar to display a temporary panel.

3 Click the Color icon to display Color panel controls (**Figure 10.9**) or click the Swatches icon to display Swatches panel controls.

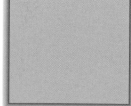

Figure 10.9 Gradient panel color controls

Figure 10.10 Creating a linear color gradient in the Gradient panel

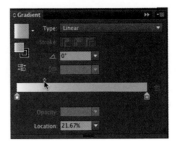

Figure 10.11 The midpoint diamond indicates where the colors in the gradient are blended equally.

4   Create a color, then click outside the temporary panel to close it.

5   Double-click the right color stop, then repeat the previous steps to specify its color.

6   From the Type menu, choose Radial or Linear (**Figure 10.10**).

7   Move the midpoint diamond (located above the gradient bar) to the right to apply more of the starting color; move it to the left to apply more of the ending color. The diamond indicates where the two colors are blended equally (**Figure 10.11**).

8   Click below the gradient bar to add a stop. Double-click the new stop and specify a color for it from the temporary panel. Move any of the midpoint diamonds to adjust how two adjacent colors are distributed in the gradient. Repeat to add more color stops (**Figure 10.12**).

9   With the custom gradient fill displayed, leave the object selected and proceed to the next task to save the custom gradient.

TIP

To remove a color stop you added, drag the stop downward off the gradient bar on the Gradient panel.

Figure 10.12 Adding a color stop to a custom gradient fill

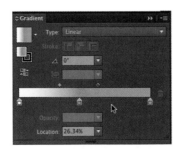

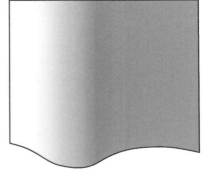

Save a Custom Gradient as a Swatch

Once you've created a custom gradient, it's best to save it as a swatch for repeated use.

Save a New Gradient

You can save a new gradient as a new swatch. To save a new gradient:

1 On the Gradient panel, display a custom gradient.

2 Do either of the following:

- Click the arrowhead to open the gradient menu. At the bottom of the menu, click the Add to Swatches icon (**Figure 10.13**). On the Swatches panel, double-click the new swatch and enter a name. Click OK.

- On the Swatches panel, click the New Swatch icon. Enter a name, then click OK.

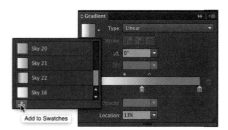

Figure 10.13 Adding your custom gradient to the Swatches panel

Modify an Existing Gradient Swatch

When you've saved and applied a gradient to an object, you can still modify the gradient and update the existing swatch. The gradient will update in all objects in the artwork to which it was applied. This updating method can be a real time-saver.

To modify a gradient:

1 Deselect all objects. Click an existing gradient swatch, then make modifications to it via the Gradient panel.

2 From the Gradient panel, Option-drag (Mac OS) or Alt-drag (Windows) the Gradient square (above the Fill and Stroke squares) over the gradient swatch on the Swatches panel. When the black drop zone frame displays around the swatch, release the mouse (**Figure 10.14**).

Any objects that contain the original gradient will update automatically.

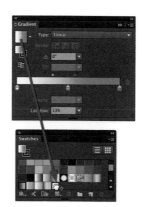

Figure 10.14 Dragging a modified custom gradient to the Swatches panel

Edit a Gradient via On-Object Controls

Sometimes, the best way to edit the colors and their exact position in a gradient is after the original gradient has been applied to an object. Working with the interactive on-object controls on the gradient annotator enables you to immediately view your modifications. How cool is that?

To edit a gradient on an object:

1   On the Gradient panel, click the Fill square.

2   Select an object, then apply a gradient fill.

3   Select the Gradient tool ▬ (G). The gradient annotator bar will display on the object. (If it doesn't, choose View > Show Gradient Annotator.)

4   Position the pointer over the bar to display the color stops (**Figure 10.15**), then do any of the following:

- Double-click a stop to modify the color via the temporary color panel you learned about earlier. Click either the Color icon (for the Color panel controls) or the Swatches icon (for the Swatches panel controls).

- To add a color stop, click below the bar (**Figure 10.16**). To modify its color, double-click the stop and use color controls on the temporary panel.

- To adjust the distribution of two adjacent colors, move a midpoint marker above the bar. To remove a stop, drag it downward off the bar.

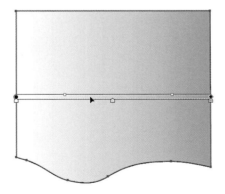

Figure 10.15 The gradient annotator bar

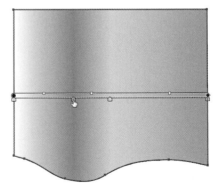

Figure 10.16 Adding a new color stop

Modify a Linear Gradient via the Annotator

The gradient annotator also provides editing methods to modify the way a linear gradient spreads across an object.

To modify a linear gradient with the annotator:

1 Select an object with a linear gradient fill.

2 Select the Gradient tool (G). The gradient annotator appears over the object.

3 Do any of the following:

- To reposition where the middle of the gradient falls within the object, drag the round endpoint in a perpendicular direction to the color bands in the gradient.

- To lengthen the overall spread of the gradient and make the transitions between colors more gradual, drag the square endpoint outward to increase the length of the bar (**Figure 10.17**). (Doing this will display less of the ending color.)

- To shorten the spread of the gradient, drag the square endpoint inward to decrease the length of the bar.

- To change the angle of the gradient, position the pointer just outside the square endpoint, then when the rotation pointer appears, drag in a circular direction (**Figure 10.18**).

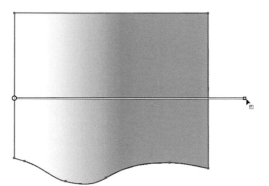

Figure 10.17 Lengthening the spread of the gradient

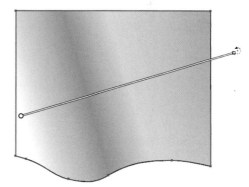

Figure 10.18 Changing the angle of the gradient

Modify a Radial Gradient via the Annotator

For a radial gradient, the gradient annotator displays a different set of editing controls. In this case, the controls enable you to modify the way gradient colors spread from the center to the edge of an object.

To modify a radial gradient with the annotator:

1   Select an object with a radial gradient fill.

2   Select the Gradient tool (G). The gradient annotator appears over the object.

3   Do any of the following:

- To reposition the gradient, drag either the bar or the larger of the two round endpoints. The center of the radial gradient does not need to remain centered on the object (**Figure 10.19**).

- To lengthen or shorten the radius of the gradient, drag the square endpoint on the bar inward or outward. This will scale the dashed ellipse and affect how gradually or abruptly colors transition in the gradient (**Figure 10.20**).

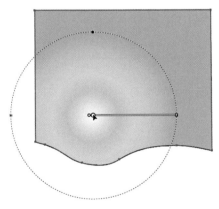

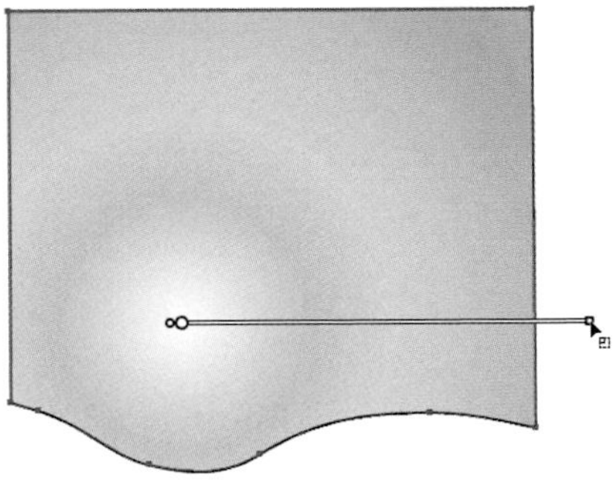

Figure 10.20 Lengthening the radius of the gradient

Figure 10.19 Repositioning the gradient

- To scale the dashed ellipse (and the radius), drag the dot with the white border on the edge of the ellipse (**Figure 10.21**).

- To change the aspect ratio of the dashed ellipse, drag the larger black dot on the ellipse inward or outward. This will make the ellipse more oval or round (**Figure 10.22**).

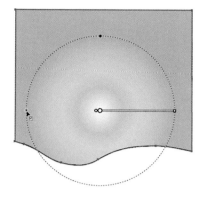

Figure 10.21 Scaling the dashed ellipse

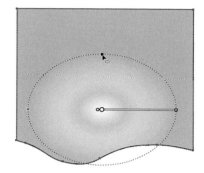

Figure 10.22 Changing the aspect ratio of the dashed ellipse

- To change the gradient angle, position the pointer on the edge of the ellipse. Then, when the rotation pointer appears, drag in a circular direction. Note that the ellipse must be more of an oval shape for you to view any angle change.

- To move the center of the radial gradient fill within the dashed ellipse, drag the smaller round endpoint on the bar away from the tiny centerpoint on the bar.

TIP

If you apply a new radial gradient to the selected object, any changes to the position, length, ratio, or angle of the annotator will be preserved.

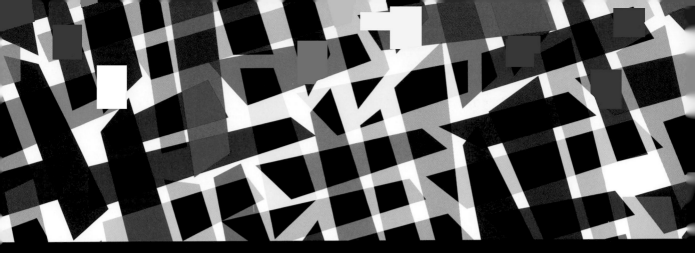

CHAPTER OBJECTIVES

Chapter Learning Objectives

- Create and edit blends.
- Release blends.
- Create shading using blends.

Chapter ACA Objectives

DOMAIN 4.0
CREATING DIGITAL GRAPHICS AND
ILLUSTRATIONS USING ADOBE ILLUSTRATOR CC

4.3 Transform graphics and illustrations.

CHAPTER 11

Creating Blends

Illustrator offers a unique way to create a multistep color and shape progression between two separate objects. The resulting object is referred to as a **blend**. In this chapter, you'll learn how to use the Blend tool to produce shape and color transitions in your artwork.

Both the Make Blend command and the Blend tool create multistep color and shape blends. Using the Blend tool, you merely click on two or more unselected objects to generate the blend. The Make Blend command generates a blend from the centers of any selected objects.

Blends are *live*. This means that the transitional objects can't be altered directly. Instead, you modify the shape, position, or color of either or both of the start and end objects in a blend and the transitional steps update automatically. You can also select a blend, then double-click the Blend tool and change the number of steps (transitions) it contains. The blend updates automatically.

Editable type objects, objects with solid color or gradient fills, and symbols (not a symbol set) can be used in a blend.

NOTE

This chapter supports the project created in Video Project 02. Go to the Video Project 02 page in the book's Web Edition to watch the entire project from beginning to end.

TIP

If you don't like the blend results, choose Edit > Undo.

NOTE

If the start or end object is a shape made from several objects (such as a robot or a face), group the objects together first, then create the blend.

TIP

If you create a blend between an object and a copy of that object at a different scale, you will create a transition in scale.

Blend Two Objects

Start your exploration of blending transitions by creating a simple blend between two objects.

1 Create two simple objects of different shapes and/or sizes. Apply different fill colors to each (**Figure 11.1**).

2 Do either of the following:

▪ Select the objects and choose Object > Blend > Make.

▪ Select the Blend tool (W), click the middle of one object, then click the middle of the other object. The objects do not need to be selected.

Illustrator creates a blend using the current Blend Options Spacing settings as shown in **Figure 11.2** (discussed in the next task).

Figure 11.1 Two simple objects with fills

Figure 11.2 Objects blended

Specify Blend Options

Any changes you make to the settings in the Blend Options dialog box will be applied automatically to any currently selected blends and applied to subsequently created blends.

1 Select an existing blend so you will be able to see your changes in action. Do either of the following:

▪ Double-click the Blend tool.

▪ Choose Object > Blend > Blend Options.

2 In the Blend Options dialog box, select Preview (**Figure 11.3**).

Figure 11.3 The Blend Options dialog box

3   From the Spacing menu, select either of the following:

- Smooth Color to have Illustrator automatically calculate the necessary number of blend steps to produce smooth, nonbanding color transitions.

- Specified Steps to enter a value for the number of transitional steps. To create a discernible transition, enter a value lower than 15. Press Tab to preview the entered value.

4   Click OK. The new options will be applied to the selected blend.

When creating a smooth color blend, try to keep your blends short (no wider than 6 inches) to minimize any color banding on print output and to minimize download speeds for web output.

Edit a Blend

Since blends are live, you can modify the start and end object at any time and the transition steps will update automatically.

Edit the Start or End Object

Use the steps below to edit one or both of the original objects in the blend.

1   Using the Selection tool ▶, double-click either the start or end object to enter isolation mode. (Objects that are not part of the blend will become dimmed and uneditable.)

2   Click either object to select it, then recolor, reposition, or transform the object (**Figures 11.4** and **11.5**). You can transform the object by dragging handles on its bounding box or by using the Free Transform tool ⬚ (E).

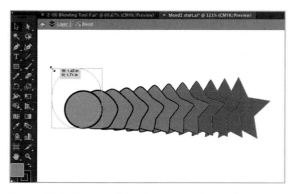

Figure 11.4 After modifying the color and scale of the start object

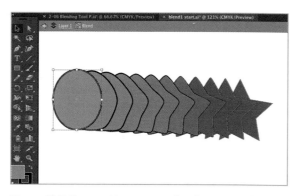

Figure 11.5 The transition steps updated automatically to reflect the edits in the blend.

TIP

If you want to change the color or position of the start or end object, you can skip isolation mode and just use the Direct Selection tool to select either object. Any change will cause the blend to update.

3 Select the Direct Selection tool ▸, then click the path of either object to reposition any points, reshape any segments, or alter any direction handles attached to a curved point.

4 Double-click a blank area of the artboard to exit isolation mode.

Transform the Entire Blend

Follow these steps to modify the entire blend object.

1 Select the blend using the Selection tool.

2 To transform the entire blend, drag any handle on its bounding box or use a transform tool.

3 To reshape the blend path (spine), do either of the following:

- To curve the path, select the Anchor Point tool (Shift+C), then drag the path to create a curved segment. You can then modify the direction handles to further modify the path.

- To add a point to the path, select the Pen tool ✐ or Add Anchor Point tool, then click the path. Use the Direct Selection tool to reposition the new point.

4 To reverse the stacking order of the blend and place the end object at the top of the stack, choose Object > Blend > Reverse Front To Back. The backmost object will now be the frontmost object.

Release a Blend

You can remove the transition steps in a blend and return to just the start and end object at any time.

1 Select a blend.

2 Choose Object > Blend > Release. The start and end objects and the path (spine) will remain, but the transition steps will be deleted.

3 Choose View > Outline, or press Command+Y (Mac OS) or Ctrl+Y (Windows), then select and delete the former path (spine) for the blend.

4 Choose View > Preview.

   Leaving the old spine may result in an accidental selection of that path when creating a new blend.

CREATING OBJECTS WITH A CUSTOM COLOR TRANSITION

If you have a color blend with a limited number of steps (**Figure 11.6**), you can convert the blend objects and the transition steps into separate objects by choosing Object > Expand. In the Expand dialog box, select all the Expand options, then click OK. The new objects will be nested within a group on the Layers panel. This is a great technique for creating objects that have a custom color transition (**Figure 11.7**).

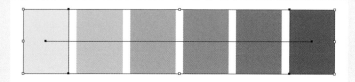

Figure 11.6 A four-step blend was created between two color objects.

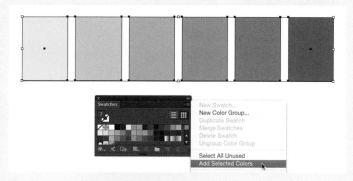

Figure 11.7 The blend was expanded. The resulting six selected color objects can now be added as swatches to the Swatches panel.

Create Shading Using Blends

▶ *Video Project*
02-05 *Work with*
Blend Steps

A more advanced way to use blends is to create the appearance of volume in a flat shape.

Add Line Shading

You can use lines to create simple hand-drawn edge shading.

1   Create a shape. Apply a fill and stroke color.

2   Use the Line Segment tool ╱ to create a short, thin line segment near the bottom of the shape.

3   Option-drag (Mac OS) or Alt-drag (Windows) to create a copy of the line segment and position the copy near the top of the shape.

4   Increase the length of either the top or bottom line segment (**Figure 11.8**).

5   Double-click the Blend tool, then set the Blend tool option for Specified Steps to between 40 and 70 steps (depending on the size of your shape). Click OK.

6   Click the Blend tool on each line segment to create the blend (**Figure 11.9**).

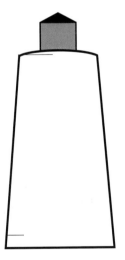

Figure 11.8 An off-white shape with a short line segment and a longer line segment placed on the left side of the shape

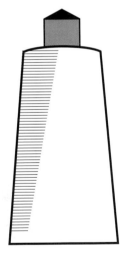

Figure 11.9 A blend of 60 steps was created using the line segments to create a shading effect.

Add Color Shading

By blending different tones of color, you can produce color shading that creates the appearance of highlight and shadow.

1 Create a shape. Apply a fill and stroke color.

2 Choose Edit > Copy to copy the shape, then use Edit > Paste In Front to place the copy directly in front of the original shape.

3 Apply a stroke of None to the copy. Scale it downward slightly to fit in the original shape. This shape will be the highlight-color object (**Figure 11.10**).

4 Create another shape for the shadow color by either drawing a new object or by modifying the width or height on a copy of the highlight object.

5 Fill the new shape with a darker tone of the large shape's original fill color. Place the new color object on one side of the large shape (**Figure 11.11**).

6 Double-click the Blend tool. In the Blend Options dialog box, select Specified Steps from the Spacing menu and enter a value between 15 and 20 steps (depending on the size of your large shape). Click OK.

7 With the Blend tool, click the shadow-color object, then click the highlight color object to create the blend (**Figure 11.12**).

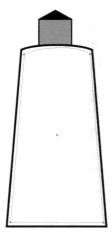

Figure 11.10 Creating the highlight-color object shape

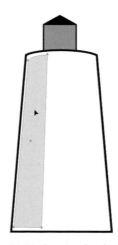

Figure 11.11 Creating the shadow color

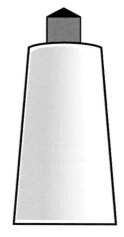

Figure 11.12 Highlight and shadow colors blended

8 Optional: To create more elaborate shading in a blend, create dark, light, and midtone color shapes. Stack the color objects as follows: dark object on top, light object in the middle, and midtone object on the bottom (**Figure 11.13**). With the Blend tool, click the dark, then light, then midtone object (**Figure 11.14**).

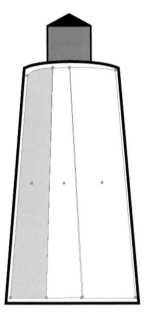

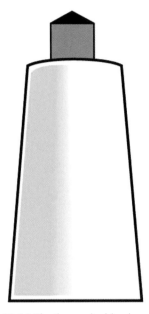

Figure 11.13 The three color tone shapes arranged from left to right in the large object

Figure 11.14 The three-color blend creates a soft highlight between the dark and midtone colors.

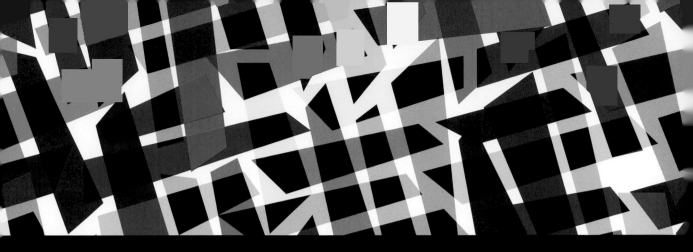

CHAPTER OBJECTIVES

Chapter Learning Objectives

- Open symbol libraries.
- Place symbols.
- Replace symbols.
- Create and edit symbols.
- Use the symbolism tools.

Chapter ACA Objectives

DOMAIN 3.0
UNDERSTANDING ADOBE ILLUSTRATOR CC

3.7 Manage brushes, symbols, graphic styles, and patterns.

DOMAIN 4.0
CREATING DIGITAL GRAPHICS AND
ILLUSTRATIONS USING ADOBE ILLUSTRATOR CC

4.2 Use vector drawing and shape tools.

CHAPTER 12

Symbols

In this chapter, you will learn how to work with symbols. **Symbols** are predefined, reusable design elements that you access via the Symbols panel in Illustrator. You'll learn how to place multiple copies of a symbol and how to modify those copies to create subtle variations within a group of symbol images. You will also get a quick overview of the eight specific symbolism tools that Illustrator provides to alter the stacking, spacing, size, angle, color tint, and transparency for a grouping (called a "set") of symbols.

Symbols are perfect for creating repetitive design elements, such as informational icons for use on a map, or the grass, flower, and tree shapes used in a landscape.

Symbols are more than just ready-made graphics—they help create more efficient files. When you place multiple copies of a symbol in a file, Illustrator defines the symbol object only once in the document code. This helps reduce file storage size and speeds up both print output and downloading times for web output. If you edit the original symbol, all occurrences of that symbol in the document will update automatically, saving you time and effort in your editing workflow.

NOTE

This chapter supports the project created in Video Project 02. Go to the Video Project 02 page in the book's Web Edition to watch the entire project from beginning to end.

★ *ACA Objective 3.7*

Open Symbol Libraries

▶ *Video Project*
02-06 Work with
Symbols

To start working with symbols, you'll open and view some symbol libraries.

1 Choose Window > Symbols to display the Symbols panel.

2 From the Symbol Libraries menu at the bottom of the Symbols panel, select a library. A floating library panel opens.

3 Do any of the following:

- Click a symbol on the library panel to place it in the Symbols panel.

- Command-click (Mac OS) or Ctrl-click (Windows) several symbols or Shift-click a series of symbols. Select Add to Symbols from the library panel menu (**Figure 12.1**).

- Drag a symbol from a library onto an artboard. The symbol will also appear on the Symbols panel.

TIP

To close a floating library panel, click the X in the upper-left corner. You can drag a floating panel into any existing dock of panels.

Figure 12.1 Selecting Add to Symbols from the Nature symbol library panel menu

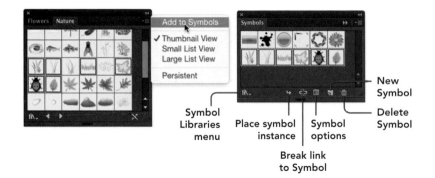

Place a Single Symbol

In the following steps, you'll place a single symbol, called an *instance*, in an Illustrator document. You will also see that an instance in your document is linked to its symbol on the Symbols panel.

1 Display the Symbols panel.

2 Do either of the following:

- Drag a symbol from the panel onto an artboard.

- Click a symbol on the panel, then click the Place Symbol Instance icon on the bottom of the panel to place it in your document.

3   Place some other symbols in your document.

4   Click each instance in your document to see its matching symbol thumbnail become selected on the Symbols panel. Note that the Break Link to Symbol icon also becomes highlighted, verifying that the instance is linked to the symbol on the panel (**Figure 12.2**).

TIP

You can apply transformations to a selected instance. To remove any transformation from a selected instance, click the Reset button on the Control panel.

Figure 12.2 When the Maple instance is selected, the Break Link to Symbol icon becomes highlighted on the Symbols panel.

Place a Set of Symbols

Here's where the fun starts with symbols. You'll use the Symbol Sprayer tool to spray multiple instances of a symbol and create a symbol set.

TIP

Command-click (Mac OS) or Ctrl-click (Windows) to quickly deselect the symbol set.

1   Select the Symbol Sprayer tool (or press Shift+S).

2   On the Symbols panel, click a symbol.

3   Click an artboard to spray one instance for each click or click and drag to quickly create multiple instances. The instances will appear in a set within one bounding box (**Figure 12.3**).

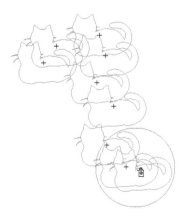
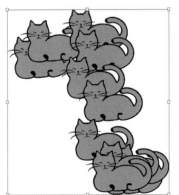

Figure 12.3 Creating multiple instances with the Symbol Sprayer tool

Add Instances to the Current Set

You can add more of the same symbol to an existing symbol set. You can also place a different symbol into an existing symbol set. This enables you to create variety within the set.

1 Select a symbol set in the document.

2 On the Symbols panel, either leave the current symbol selected (to add more of the same one) or click a different symbol.

3 Drag with the Symbol Sprayer tool to add more symbols (**Figure 12.4**).

Figure 12.4 Selecting a different symbol and adding it to the symbol set

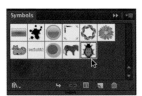
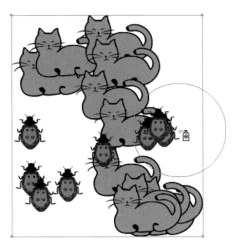

Remove Instances from the Current Set

Just as you can add instances to a set, you can also remove instances. To remove a symbol instance from a set:

1 Select a symbol set in the document.

2 On the Symbols panel, click the symbol you want to remove from the set. (If the set was created from one symbol, that symbol will be selected on the Symbols panel.)

3 Select the Symbol Sprayer tool or press Shift+S. Option-click (Mac OS) or Alt-click (Windows) or Option-drag/Alt-drag over symbols in the set.

Replace a Symbol

The Control panel and Symbols panel each provides an easy method for replacing symbols. To replace a symbol, do either of the following:

NOTE

The Replace Symbol feature replaces all the symbols in a set, even if the set contains different symbols.

- Select an individual instance in your artwork. On the Control panel, click the Replace thumbnail arrowhead to open a temporary Symbols panel, then click a replacement symbol.

- Select a symbol set in your artwork. On the Symbols panel, click a replacement symbol, then choose Replace Symbol from the panel menu (**Figures 12.5** and **12.6**).

Figure 12.5 With the maple leaf symbol selected on the Symbols panel, select Replace Symbol from the panel menu.

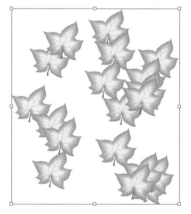

Figure 12.6 The former symbols in the set are replaced by the maple leaf symbol.

Create a Symbol

TIP

To delete a symbol that is not used in the document, select it on the Symbols panel. Click the Delete Symbol icon on the bottom of the Symbols panel, then click Yes to confirm the deletion.

One or more Illustrator objects can be made into a symbol. If you're planning to spray your custom symbol densely all over your artwork, try to avoid creating the symbol from complex objects to avoid a performance slowdown in Illustrator. The object for your symbol can be an open or closed path, a group, or type. It can contain a brush stroke or effect.

1. Create one or more objects. Color and scale them as desired. Using the Selection tool ▸, Shift-click to select all the objects.

2. On the bottom of the Symbols panel, click the New Symbol icon (**Figure 12.7**).

3. In the Symbol Options dialog box, enter a name for the symbol.

4. If your file will be exported to Adobe Flash, select Movie Clip or Graphic from the Export Type menu. If the symbol will be used for web output, select Align to Pixel Grid to prevent blurry line edges.

TIP

To delete a symbol that is used in the document, select it on the Symbols panel and click the Delete Symbol icon. Then, click Expand Instances to create standard, unlinked objects or click Delete Instances to delete all linked instances of the symbol.

5. Click OK. The symbol appears on the Symbols panel (**Figure 12.8**).

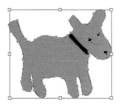
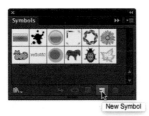

Figure 12.7 Click the New Symbol icon.

Figure 12.8 The new dog symbol appears on the Symbols panel.

Edit a Symbol

You can easily edit a symbol that is either on the Symbols panel or placed as an instance in your document. Any edits will be applied automatically to any instances and sets in the document.

1. To edit a symbol, do either of the following:
   - Double-click a symbol on the Symbols panel. A temporary instance of the symbol will be placed in isolation mode.

- Click an individual symbol instance in the document, then click the Edit Symbol button on the Control panel. Click OK in the alert. The symbol will be placed in isolation mode.

2   Edit the object or objects as shown in **Figure 12.9** (for example, recolor, reshape, or transform).

3   Press Esc to exit isolation mode. Any edits will be applied to the original symbol on the panel and to any instances that are linked to the symbol (**Figure 12.10**).

If you want to edit a copy of an existing symbol, select it on the Symbols panel, select Duplicate Symbol from the panel menu, then follow the steps described in this section.

Figure 12.9 A doggie symbol instance being edited in isolation mode. The symbol is also contained in a symbol set.

Figure 12.10 After exiting isolation mode, the edits to the symbol are automatically applied to all instances.

Symbolism Tools

You have already worked with the Symbol Sprayer tool to create symbol sets. With the other seven symbolism tools, you can modify the stacking, spacing, and appearance of instances in a selected set.

To use a tool, click an instance or drag across a symbol set. A symbol tool's effect is strongest in the center of its brush cursor and diminishes gradually toward the brush perimeter.

If a selected symbol set contains more than one type of symbol, select the symbol you want to modify on the Symbols panel. Any tool edits will be limited to only those instances.

Symbolism Tool Options

The eight symbolism tools share the same Symbolism Tools Options dialog box.

- **Global tool settings:** The upper part of the dialog box provides settings and options that are global and apply to all eight tools.

- **Tool selection:** The middle part of the dialog box displays a row of icons for selecting one of the eight tools and switching to its specific panel.

- **Tool shortcuts and modifiers:** The lower part of the dialog box displays specific options or modifier key shortcuts that apply to the currently selected tool.

You'll examine the global options here.

1 Double-click any symbolism tool to open the Symbolism Tools Options dialog box (**Figure 12.11**).

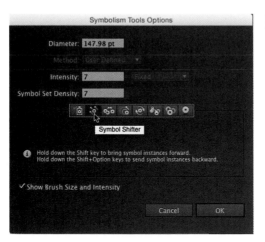

Figure 12.11 The Symbolism Tools Options dialog box

2 To specify a default brush size for all the symbolism tools, enter a Diameter value. You can also decrease/increase the brush size interactively in the document window by pressing the Left Bracket ([) or Right Bracket (]) key.

3 To control the rate at which the Symbol Sprayer tool places instances (or the other tools apply their adjustment), enter an Intensity value. The higher the value, the greater the tool effect.

4 To specify how tightly all the instances will be packed within a set, enter a Symbol Set Density value. The higher the value, the tighter the packing.

5 Select Show Brush Size And Intensity to have Illustrator represent the tool diameter setting as a ring around the tool icon and represent the Intensity setting as a shade of gray (black for high intensity, light gray for low intensity).

6 Click OK.

NOTE

A change in this option will automatically affect any currently selected symbol set.

Symbolism Tool Specifics

Following is a brief overview of each of the remaining seven symbolism tools. Remember to select a symbol set before using any of these tools (**Figure 12.12**).

 ACA Objective 4.2

Figure 12.12 The initial symbol set before applying any symbolism tool modifications

Symbol Shifter Tool

The Symbol Shifter tool  has two functions. The tool shifts instances slightly in the direction you drag. Shift-click to bring an instance in front of the others; Option-Shift-click (Mac OS) or Alt-Shift-click (Windows) to send an instance behind the others (**Figure 12.13**).

Figure 12.13 Shifting the position of symbols with the Symbol Shifter tool

Symbol Scruncher Tool

The Symbol Scruncher tool ⚙ affects the distance between instances. Click and hold on a set to pull instances together. Option-click (Mac OS) or Alt-click (Windows) to push instances apart (**Figure 12.14**).

Figure 12.14 Pulling and pushing instances with the Symbol Scruncher tool

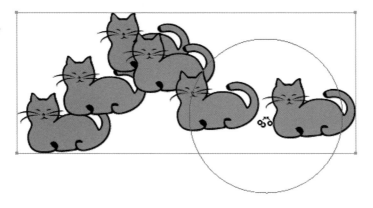

Symbol Sizer Tool

The Symbol Sizer tool ⚙ scales instances by variable amounts. Click an instance or drag across instances to enlarge some of them. Option-click (Mac OS) or Alt-click (Windows) or Option-drag/Alt-drag to shrink instances (**Figure 12.15**).

Figure 12.15 Creating variable sizes with the Symbol Sizer tool

Symbol Spinner Tool

The Symbol Spinner tool ⟳ rotates instances. As you drag, temporary arrows designate the direction of rotation being applied (**Figure 12.16**).

Figure 12.16 Rotating symbols with the Symbol Spinner tool

Symbol Stainer Tool

The Symbol Stainer tool 🧪 colorizes solid-color, pattern, and gradient fills contained in instances. Variable tints of the current fill color will be applied (**Figure 12.17**). The lightness or darkness of the original color will be preserved. The results create complex groups of objects.

TIP

For more control over recoloring instances in a symbol set, use the Recolor Artwork feature.

Figure 12.17 Modifying the color of instances with the Symbol Stainer tool

Symbol Screener Tool

The Symbol Screener tool creates a fade effect by applying different levels of transparency to instances. Option-click (Mac OS) or Alt-click (Windows) or Option-drag/Alt-drag to restore the full opacity of instances (**Figure 12.18**).

Figure 12.18 Creating a fade effect with the Symbol Screener tool

Symbol Styler Tool

The Symbol Styler tool enables you to quickly apply a graphic style. It does this by applying to instances the appearances from the currently selected graphic style thumbnail on the Graphic Styles panel (**Figure 12.19**). The effect can be rather hit-or-miss depending on the appearances in the selected style. It's probably best to initially use this tool on a symbol with solid color as a way to apply additional styling. The results create complex groups of objects with appearances. Avoid using this tool if your artwork will be exported for web output.

Figure 12.19 The Symbol Styler tool applies the selected style from the Graphic Styles panel.

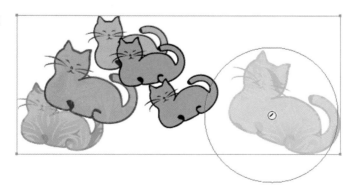

Unlink or Expand Instances

To break the link between instances (standalone or in a symbol set) and the original symbol, first select an instance or set on the Symbols panel. Then, click the Break Link to Symbol icon on the Symbols panel or Control panel. Breaking the link will convert the instances to standard objects or groups of objects.

The Object > Expand command will break a symbol set into separate instances that are still linked to the original symbol. When this command is applied again to those selected, individual instances, the link to the original symbol will be broken and the instances will be converted to standard objects nested within a group.

Use either of these methods when you want to prevent a symbol set from being modified when editing the symbol it was based on. You can also apply these methods when you want to use standard Illustrator tools and panels to edit, recolor, or reposition elements in the set.

Save a Custom Symbol Library

After you've created your own user-defined symbols and added symbols from some of the predefined libraries to the Symbols panel, you can save all of the symbols on the panel to a custom library.

1 Create some custom symbols or edit some predefined symbols.

2 Add symbols from some of the predefined libraries to the Symbols panel.

3 On the bottom of the Symbols panel, click the Symbol Libraries menu icon, then select Save Symbols from the menu.

4 In the Save Symbols As Library dialog box, enter a name, leave the location as the Symbols folder, then click Save.

TIP

You can access your saved library from any open Illustrator document by clicking the Symbol Libraries menu icon and selecting the User Defined category at the bottom of the menu.

CHAPTER OBJECTIVES

Chapter Learning Objectives

- Draw with the Pen tool.
- Convert points on a path.
- Add or remove points on a path.
- Cut and join paths.
- Trace a raster image.
- Draw with the Pencil tool.

Chapter ACA Objectives

DOMAIN 3.0
UNDERSTANDING ADOBE ILLUSTRATOR CC

3.2 Define the functions of commonly used tools, including selection tools, the Pen tool, and other drawing tools, shape tools and transformation tools.

3.9 Demonstrate an understanding of vector drawing tools.

DOMAIN 4.0
CREATING DIGITAL GRAPHICS AND ILLUSTRATIONS USING ADOBE ILLUSTRATOR CC

4.3 Transform graphics and illustrations.

CHAPTER 13

Pen and Pencil Tools

In this chapter, you will learn how to work with the Pen tool and the Pencil tool—two important drawing tools in Illustrator that enable you to draw the twists and turns in the path of a custom shape.

The Pen tool is one of the most powerful tools in the program. It is also one of the more difficult tools to learn. You use the tool to place anchor points and draw the straight or curved segments between points. As you start to work with this tool, remember that you can always go back and tweak the path shape by moving points and readjusting curved segments—techniques that you have already learned.

The Pencil tool enables you to draw in a freehand manner to sketch a shape. The tool will create both the points and segments on the freehand paths you draw.

NOTE

This chapter supports the project created in Video Project 03. Go to the Video Project 03 page in the book's Web Edition to watch the entire project from beginning to end.

Draw with the Pen Tool

The Pen tool creates precise curved and straight segments that are connected to anchor points. You can either click with the tool to create corner points and straight segments or drag with the tool to create smooth points and curved segments. When you drag, you are actually determining the length of the direction handles that define a curve.

★ *ACA Objective 3.2*

★ *ACA Objective 3.9*

▶ *Video Project 03-01 The Pen Tool*

Straight-Sided Paths

The easier way to draw with the Pen tool is by clicking to create a straight-sided object.

1 Select the Pen tool (P) .

2 Make sure View > Smart Guides is enabled to display temporary alignment guides while drawing.

3 Click to create the first anchor point. Reposition the pointer to place the second anchor point. The Rubber Band path preview option will visualize the next straight segment (**Figure 13.1**).

4 Click to create a second point and a straight segment (**Figure 13.2**).

Figure 13.1 The first anchor point created with the first pen click

Figure 13.2 The second anchor point created

TIP

To reposition a point while you are creating it, hold down the spacebar, drag to move the point, then release the spacebar.

5 Click to create additional anchor points (**Figure 13.3**).

Figure 13.3 More pen clicks create more anchor points.

6 To complete the shape, do either of the following:

■ To complete the object as an open path and deselect it, Command-click (Mac OS) or Ctrl-click (Windows) away from the object, or press Esc.

■ To complete the object as a closed path, position the pointer over the starting point (a tiny circle appears by the pointer and an "anchor" label appears next to the point), then click the point.

NOTE *The Pen tool pointer will display an asterisk* ✎* *to indicate that the tool is ready to create a new path.*

Curved Paths

When you drag the Pen tool, you will create an anchor point with a smooth curve and a pair of direction handles. If you rotate one direction handle for a smooth curve anchor point, the other handle moves in tandem to preserve the smoothness of both curved segments attached to the point.

1 Select the Pen tool and make sure that View > Smart Guides is enabled.

2 Drag to create the first anchor point. Two direction handles appear, aligned with the direction you drag. Release the mouse.

3 Position the tool pointer where you want the next point. The Rubber Band path preview option will visualize the next curved segment (**Figure 13.4**).

4 To place the second anchor point, drag in the direction you want the curved segment to follow. The more you drag, the longer the direction handles you are creating will be. Release the mouse (**Figure 13.5**).

TIP

To produce smooth, symmetrical curves, place the points at the beginning and end of each arc rather than at the middle. This will prevent creating a potential bump on the smooth curve. The curve will also be easier to edit because there will be only two direction handles controlling the segment.

Figure 13.4 The next curve segment is visualized.

Figure 13.5 The second anchor point is placed.

5 Drag to create more anchor points and direction handles (**Figure 13.6**).

6 Do either of the following:

- To complete the object as an open path and deselect it, Command-click (Mac OS) or Ctrl-click (Windows) away from the object, or press Esc.

- To complete the object as a closed path, position the pointer over the starting point. A tiny circle indicator appears by the pointer and an "anchor" label appears next to the point. Then drag to create the last pair of direction handles.

TIP

A path can contain a combination of straight and curved segments. As you draw, you can click to create corner points, then click and drag to create smooth points.

Figure 13.6 More anchor points and direction handles are created.

Non-Smooth Curved Paths

The Pen tool can also create non-smooth curves—curved segments that jut out from the same side of an anchor point. Direction handles for this type of point move independently of each other. Rotating one handle does not affect the other handle. You can determine whether a point will be smooth or non-smooth while you are drawing.

1   Select the Pen tool.

2   Drag to create the first curved anchor point. Release the mouse.

3   Position the tool pointer where you want the next point.

    The Rubber Band path preview will visualize the next curved segment.

4   To place the second anchor point, drag in the direction you want the curved segment to follow. Without releasing the mouse, hold down Option (Mac OS) or Alt (Windows), then reposition the direction handle under the pointer to create a V shape with its paired handle. Release the mouse (**Figure 13.7**).

5   Position the pointer to place the third point. The Rubber Band preview shows that a matching arc will be created. Drag to create the curve for that point (**Figure 13.8**).

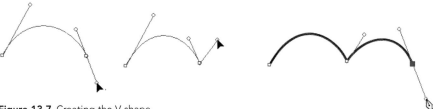

Figure 13.7 Creating the V shape

Figure 13.8 Creating a second curve

6   Repeat steps 4 and 5 to place additional points and adjust the handles.

7   To close the shape, do any of the following:

    ▪ Position the pointer over the starting point, then drag to create a smooth point.

    ▪ Click the starting point to convert it to a corner point with one direction handle.

    ▪ Position the pointer over the starting point. Hold down Option (Mac OS) or Alt (Windows), then drag and rotate the pointer to force the direction handle to create a V shape with its paired handle. (This will initially feel awkward; with practice you'll become more adept at it.) Release the mouse.

Add Segments

You can add segments to an open path at any time using the Pen tool.

1 Select the Pen tool. Position the pointer over the endpoint of a selected or unselected open path. A forward slash (/) indicator displays next to the pointer (**Figure 13.9**).

2 Do any of the following (**Figure 13.10**):

- Click the highlighted point to create a corner point, then move the pointer and click to create another corner point.

- Click and drag to create a direction handle for a curve point. Move the pointer, then drag to create a smooth curve.

- Click and drag, then Option-drag (Mac OS) or Alt-drag (Windows) the direction handle to create a non-smooth curve. Move the pointer, then drag to create a non-smooth curve.

Figure 13.9 Preparing to add a segment to a corner point (left). Preparing to add a segment to a curved point (right).

Figure 13.10 Adding straight and curved segments to a path

Convert Points

The points on a path can be converted from corner to curved or from curved to cor- ner at any time. This feature enables you to initially draw rough shapes composed of all corner points or all curved points, and then go back and adjust individual points to create the desired path or shape. This is probably the most common way to create complex paths in Illustrator.

★ *ACA Objective 4.3*

Convert Using the Direct Selection Tool

As you have learned in the chapters that covered reshaping paths, the Direct Selection tool can be used to convert points.

1 Select the Direct Selection tool ▶, then click the edge of a path.

2 Do either of the following (**Figure 13.11**):

- Option-drag (Mac OS) or Alt-drag (Windows) a direction handle to convert a smooth curve into a non-smooth curve with independent direction handles.

- Click a point on a path to select it. On the Control panel, click the Convert Selected Anchor Points to Corner icon ▐ or the Convert Selected Anchor Points to Smooth icon ▐.

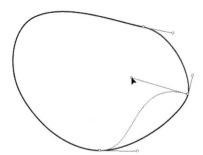

Figure 13.11 Converting a smooth curve to a non-smooth curve

Convert via Anchor Point Tool

The Anchor Point tool, located in the same tool group as the Pen tool, can also be used to convert points.

1 Select the Anchor Point tool (Shift-C).

2 Click a curved point to convert it to a corner point and remove the direction handles.

3 Drag on and away from a corner point to convert it to a smooth point and create direction handles (**Figure 13.12**).

NOTE *You can also drag a selected curved segment with the Direct Selection tool to reshape it. If you drag a selected straight segment with this tool, that side of the shape will extend and a curve segment will not be created.*

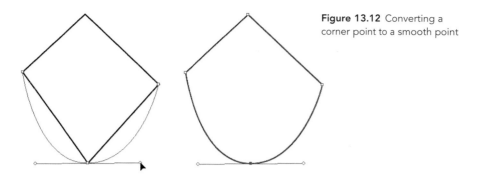

Figure 13.12 Converting a corner point to a smooth point

Add or Remove Points

The Pen tool has yet another function: adding or removing points from a path. Below is a quick overview of these features. (You learned how to use the Pen tool to remove points at the end of Chapter 3.)

To add a point to a selected path, roll the Pen tool over a segment, then click when the plus sign (+) indicator appears by the pointer. (You could also click with the Add Anchor Point tool, located in the same tool group as the Pen tool.) Press A to select the Direct Selection tool, then drag the new anchor point to reshape the path.

To remove a selected point from a path, roll the Pen tool over the point, then click when the minus sign (–) indicator displays by the pointer. (You could also click with the Delete Anchor Point tool ✒, located in the same tool group as the Pen tool, or click the Remove Selected Anchor Points icon on the Control panel.)

Cut and Join Paths

Another way to modify an existing path is to cut it, thereby creating either an open path with two endpoints or breaking an existing open path into two paths.

Cut a Path

Follow these steps to cut a path. After a path has been cut open, you can use the Pen tool to add new segments to the path.

TIP

When you cut open a closed path, any stroke will display a gap, but any fill will be preserved.

1 Do either of the following:

   ■ Press A to select the Direct Selection tool, then click an anchor point on a closed or open path. On the Control panel, click the Cut Path At Selected Anchor Points icon.

   ■ Choose the Scissors tool (C) ✂. Click on a segment or an anchor point on a selected or unselected path.

   Two nonconnected anchor points will be created and stacked on top of each other.

2 Using the Direct Selection tool, drag one of the anchor points away to view the open path (**Figure 13.13**).

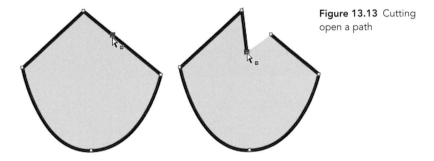

Figure 13.13 Cutting open a path

Join Two Endpoints

The Join tool is used to unite (join) two endpoints on an open path (to close the path) or on two separate paths (to join the two paths into one path).

TIP

If the endpoints do not join, try moving them closer together, then try the Join tool again.

1 Position two endpoints from one path (or from two different paths) close to each other. Make sure both paths are in the same state, either selected or deselected.

2 Select the Join tool ⟿ (located in the tool group under the Pencil tool ✏).

3 Scrub (drag) across both endpoints. A color line indicator appears.

4 Release the mouse. The points are joined into one point.

Manually Trace a Raster Image

A common task in Illustrator is to use the Pen tool to manually trace the edges of a raster image to produce a clean, sharp-edge vector version of the image. Raster images are composed of pixels with soft, subtle transitions between shapes in the image. Raster images are good for reproducing continuous-tone photographs, but not good for producing sharp-edged artwork.

When tracing a raster image, place the image on its own top-level layer, then use the Transparency panel to lower the Opacity for the image to 50%. Next, on the Layers panel, click the blank slot to the left of that layer listing to lock it; this prevents objects on the layer from being selected. The lock icon appears in the slot. Click the lock icon to unlock the layer and remove the icon.

After locking the raster image layer, use the Pen tool to create closed paths that follow the edges of color areas in the image. Use the Eyedropper tool ✐ (I) to sample colors from the areas in the image, then apply those colors to the path objects you have created (**Figure 13.14**).

▶ **Video Project
03-02** Trace an Image with the Pen Tool

NOTE

If you double-click a top-level layer listing and select Template in the Layer Options dialog box, any images on that layer will be dimmed and all objects on that layer will be locked.

 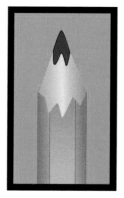

Figure 13.14 The original raster image (left). The vector shapes created with the Pen tool (right).

Draw with the Pencil Tool

The Pencil tool gives you the chance to show off your drawing skills. You can drag the Pencil tool to create a freehand sketch consisting of open or closed paths. As with any path in Illustrator, you can go back later and reshape segments and reposition points to tweak your shape.

1 Select the Pencil tool (N) ✐.
2 Specify a stroke color and weight (width), and a fill color of None.

▶ **Video Project
03-03** Freehand Drawing with the Pencil Tool

▶ **Video Project
03-04** Trace a Photo with the Pencil Tool

3   Draw lines. A preview line will follow your mouse movements. Release the mouse between strokes. That's all there is to it (**Figure 13.15**).

4   To create a closed path with the Pencil tool, draw a path that returns to its starting point and release the mouse when a tiny circle indicator displays by the tool pointer.

If the circle indicator does not display, see the next section, "Set Pencil Tool Options."

TIP *To draw a perfectly straight horizontal or vertical line, Shift-drag the Pencil tool. To draw straight segments within a freehand line, hold down Option (Mac OS) or Alt (Windows) as you drag the tool. Release the modifier key and continue to drag to draw freehand again. In each method, an underscore (_) indicator will appear by the pointer.*

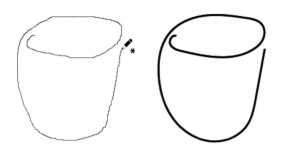

Figure 13.15 Shaping segments with the Pencil tool

Set Pencil Tool Options

The Pencil tool's behavior can be customized via its Tool Options dialog box. You can adjust how smoothly or accurately a Pencil line follows your freehand movements and control whether the tool can reshape existing paths. Changes to the Pencil Tool Options affect only subsequent path you draw, not existing paths.

1   Double-click the Pencil tool icon, or press Return (Mac OS) or Enter (Windows) if the tool is already selected.

The Pencil Tool Options dialog box opens.

2   In the Fidelity area, drag the slider toward Accurate (to precisely follow the mouse movements and increase the number of points on a drawn path) or toward Smooth (to loosely follow mouse movements and decrease the number of points on a drawn path).

3 Under Options, select any of the following:

- Fill New Pencil Strokes to automatically apply the current fill color to new paths.

- Keep Selected to have a new path stay selected. This can save you a step if you tend to edit each path immediately after creating it.

- Option Key Toggles To Smooth Tool (Alt on Windows) to enable keyboard shortcut access to the Smooth tool.

- Close Paths When Ends Are Within [entered value] to determine within what distance the tool will sense the starting point of the current path.

- Edit Selected Paths to activate the reshaping function of the tool (see the next section). Use the Within slider to determine the maximum distance the tool must be from a path to be able to reshape it.

4 Click OK.

TIP

Click Reset in the Pencil Tool Options dialog box to restore the default settings for the tool.

Reshape Using the Pencil Tool

You can also use the Pencil tool to quickly reshape a portion of any selected path, regardless of which tool or command was used to create the path.

1 Position the Pencil tool over a portion of a selected open or closed path.

2 Drag to reshape the path (**Figure 13.16**).

- For an open path, you can finish up either on the path (to modify a portion of the path) or off the path (to redraw that whole end of the path).

- For a closed path, you must finish up on another part of the path to avoid creating a new path instead.

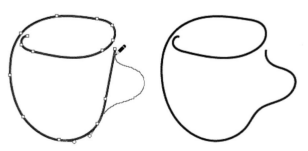

Figure 13.16 Dragging to reshape a path with the Pencil tool

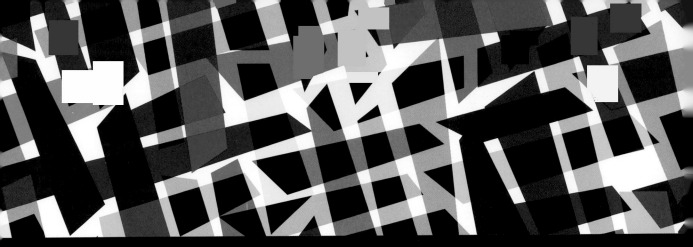

CHAPTER OBJECTIVES

Chapter Learning Objectives

- Learn about the Brushes panel.
- Apply brushes.
- Edit brushes.
- Create custom brushes.
- Use the Blob Brush.

Chapter ACA Objectives

DOMAIN 3.0
UNDERSTANDING ADOBE ILLUSTRATOR CC

3.7 Manage brushes, symbols, graphic styles, and patterns.

3.9 Demonstrate an understanding of vector drawing tools.

DOMAIN 4.0
CREATING DIGITAL GRAPHICS AND ILLUSTRATIONS USING ADOBE ILLUSTRATOR CC

4.2 Use vector drawing and shape tools.

CHAPTER 14

Brushes

In this chapter, you will learn how to work with brushes to apply different looks to a stroke, including ink, paint, chalk, patterns, or an image. You will learn about the five different categories of brushes that are available in Illustrator and how to paint brushstrokes using the Paintbrush tool.

Even though brushes produce the look of painterly texture, they're still vector graphics, so your file sizes will remain small and your artwork will print and display onscreen with sharp edges.

Brushes are also editable. You can change certain properties for a brush that's being used in your artwork and have those changes update automatically on all occurrences of the brush. If you reshape a path or increase its stroke width, any applied brush will conform to those changes.

NOTE

This chapter supports the project created in Video Project 03. Go to the Video Project 03 page in the book's Web Edition to watch the entire project from beginning to end.

The Brushes Panel

★ *ACA Objective 3.7*

▶ *Video Project 03-05 Apply a Brush*

The Brushes panel shows the default set of brushes and any brushes you have added from brush libraries or have created from custom objects. The Brushes panel lists brushes from top to bottom in five specific categories (**Figure 14.1**):

- **Calligraphic:** Thin and thick contours on a path
- **Scatter:** Shapes that are scattered on or around a path
- **Art:** Graphic shapes or images that are applied along a path
- **Bristle:** Shades of color that mimic the bristle look of traditional art media
- **Pattern:** A collection of graphic tiles that produce a stylish border or frame along the path

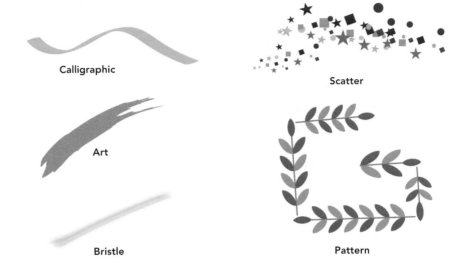

Figure 14.1 The five brush strokes in the Brushes panel: Calligraphic, Scatter, Art, Bristle, and Pattern

Calligraphic

Scatter

Art

Bristle

Pattern

TIP

On the bottom of the floating library panel, click the Load Next Brush Library or Load Previous Brush Library icon to view other libraries of brushes.

The first step in working with brushes is to add a variety of brushes to the various categories on the Brushes panel (**Figure 14.2**).

1 Deselect all objects.

2 Choose Window > Brushes to display the Brushes panel.

3 Click the Brush Libraries menu icon at the bottom of the panel, and select a library from a category submenu.

4 In the floating panel that opens, Command-click (Mac OS) or Ctrl-click (Windows) some brushes, then select Add to Brushes from the panel menu.

The new brushes are listed on the Brushes panel in their respective category.

Figure 14.2 The Brushes panel

Calligraphic brushes

Scatter brushes

Art brushes

Bristle brush

Pattern brush

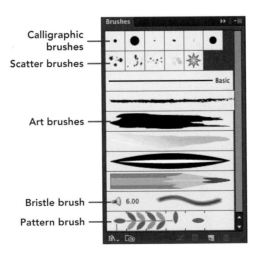

Apply Brushes

Now that you have some brushes in the Brushes panel, you can apply a brush to an existing path.

1 Select an object in your document.

2 To select a brush, click one in the Brushes panel or select one from the Brush Definition menu on the Control panel.

   The brush is applied to the path.

3 Change the stroke width to enlarge the path (**Figure 14.3**).

4 *Optional*: Select a different brush to change the selected brush stroke.

Figure 14.3 From left to right: The original stroke; a brush applied to the stroke; the stroke width increased

Paint a Brush Stroke

Use the Paintbrush tool to draw a brush stroke on an artboard.

★ *ACA Objective 4.2*

1 Select the Paintbrush tool 🖌 (B).

2 Click a brush on the Brushes panel or select one from the Brush Definition menu on the Control panel. Apply a fill of None, a stroke color, and a stroke width.

3 Drag the Paintbrush tool across an artboard.

4 *Optional*: Select a different brush to change the selected brush stroke.

> **TIP** *To draw a closed brush path, draw a path that comes back near the starting point, then hold down Option (Mac OS) or Alt (Windows) and release the mouse button. The end of the brush stroke may not necessarily overlap the start (**Figure 14.4**).*

Figure 14.4 A closed brush path

Remove a Brush Stroke

You can remove a brush stroke from a path at any time. To remove a brush stroke:

1 Select an object that has a brush applied to its stroke.

2 Do either of the following:

   ■ On the Brushes panel, click the Remove Brush Stroke icon on the bottom of the panel (**Figure 14.5**).

   ■ On the Brushes panel or on the Brush Definition menu (Control panel), select the Basic brush option.

Figure 14.5 Removing a brush stroke

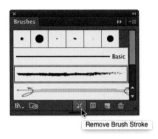

▶ *Video Project*
03-07 *Create/Edit*
Brushes

TIP

For any Brush Options dialog box that provides a Colorization option, select Method: Tints to enable applying the current Stroke color as a tint to the brush stroke.

Edit Brushes

Illustrator offers specific options and settings that control the properties of each type of brush. Those options and settings, in turn, can be edited in one of five specific Brush Options dialog boxes. Following is a simple overview of editing the properties for four of the five different brush categories.

> **TIP** *To modify the colors of objects in any brush that's applied to a selected path, use the Recolor Artwork option on the Control panel. Edits will affect only the selected brush stroke (not the brush on the Brushes panel).*

Edit a Calligraphic Brush

Settings for a calligraphic brush focus on altering the angle and roundness of the brush shape.

1 Select an object that has a calligraphic brush applied to its stroke.

2 On the Brushes panel, double-click the highlighted calligraphic brush thumbnail to edit it.

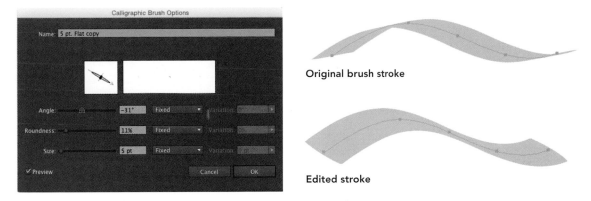

Original brush stroke

Edited stroke

Figure 14.6 The Calligraphic Brush Options dialog box with new Angle and Roundness settings

3 In the Calligraphic Brush Options dialog box, select Preview to view your changes (**Figure 14.6**).

4 Adjust the Angle slider to determine where thin and thick areas are on the stroke.

5 Set the Roundness slider to a low value for a narrow, thin tip to create a thin and thick brush stroke, and keep the Size value low (you will use stroke width to control brush size).

6 View your changes in the preview and on the selected brush stroke. Click OK, then click Apply to Strokes.

Edit a Scatter Brush

Editing a scatter brush involves modifying the size, spacing, and proximity to the path for the objects in the brush.

1 Select an object that has a scatter brush applied to its stroke.

2 On the Brushes panel, double-click the highlighted scatter brush thumbnail to edit it.

3 In the Scatter Brush Options dialog box, select Preview to see your changes (**Figure 14.7**).

4 Adjust the settings for Size (of scatter objects), Spacing (distance between the scatter objects), Scatter (distance of objects from the path), and Rotation (rotation of scatter objects).

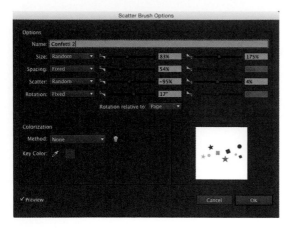

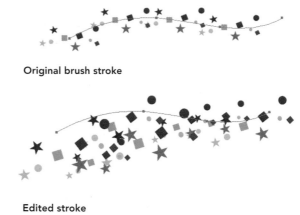

Original brush stroke

Edited stroke

Figure 14.7 The Scatter Brush Options dialog box with new Size, Spacing, and Scatter settings

5 If any option is set to Random, you can drag its sliders to determine the minimum and maximum value possible for that setting.

6 View your changes on the selected brush stroke. Click OK, then click Apply to Strokes.

Edit an Art Brush

Options for an art brush focus on how the graphic (art) object that is used in the brush will be scaled on a path.

Figure 14.8 A vector drawing of a pencil was used to create a new art brush.

1 Select an object that has an art brush applied to its stroke (**Figure 14.8**).

2 On the Brushes panel, double-click the highlighted art brush thumbnail to edit it.

3 In the Art Brush Options dialog box, select Preview to see your changes (**Figure 14.9**).

4 Select a Brush Scale Option:

- **Scale Proportionately** preserves the original proportions of the art object.

- **Stretch To Fit Stroke Length** allows Illustrator to stretch (distort) the art object to fit the path.

- **Stretch Between Guides** allows you to move the dashed guides in the preview to define which part of the art object Illustrator can stretch and which part will be preserved (not stretched).

5 View your changes on the selected brush stroke. Click OK, then click Apply to Strokes.

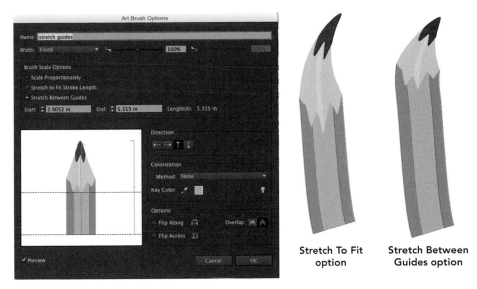

Stretch To Fit
option

Stretch Between
Guides option

Figure 14.9 The Art Brush Options dialog box with the Stretch Between Guides scale option selected. Notice that the upper dashed guide has been placed below the pencil tip.

Edit a Pattern Brush

A pattern brush is composed of up to five tiles, each placed on a specific part of a path (outer corner, inner corner, side, start, or end). Editing the brush involves choosing imagery for each tile and determining how the tiles are scaled on a path.

1   Create art objects to be used as substitute tiles for the sides, corners, start, and end parts of an existing pattern brush. Drag each tile object separately into the Swatches panel.

2   Apply the pattern brush you want to edit to an object, and keep the object selected.

3   On the Brushes panel, double-click the highlighted pattern brush thumbnail to edit it.

The Pattern Brush Options dialog box displays five tile thumbnails, each with a menu and a diagram of where that tile will be used on a path.

4   Click a tile thumbnail, then choose one of your new pattern swatches from the menu. Do this for each substitute tile part you created (**Figure 14.10**).

> **NOTE** Start and end tiles are applied only to an open path (not a closed path).

TIP

To create corner tiles automatically, replace only the side tile with new artwork. Then, click each of the two corner tile thumbnails to display a menu and select Show Auto Generated Corner Tiles. You can then select from the Auto-Centered, Auto-Between, Auto-Sliced, and Auto-Overlap options.

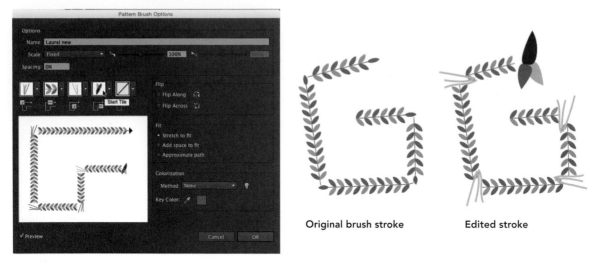

Original brush stroke   Edited stroke

Figure 14.10 The Pattern Brush Options dialog box with new Outer Corner, Inner Corner, and Start Tile artwork

5 Click a Fit option to determine how the pattern is adjusted to fit a path.

6 View your changes in the preview area at lower left. (Sorry, these edits do not preview on the selected object.) Click OK, then click Apply to Strokes.

> **TIP** *To create a pattern stroke that displays corner tiles, use the Pen or Pencil tool (rather than the Paintbrush tool) to draw a path with straight segments and sharp corner points.*

Create a Watercolor Wash Effect

You can use watercolor brushes (accessed from the Artistic_Watercolor brush library) to paint strokes of different color tints on a separate layer stacked behind a line art sketch.

▶ *Video Project 03-06 Watercolor Effect*

You can paint using colors from the Swatches panel or you can use the Eyedropper tool ✐ to sample a color from any placed photographic image, then paint with the sampled color. Consider saving the sampled color as a swatch.

Create a Custom Brush

Now that you know how to draw and reshape objects in Illustrator, it's easy to apply those skills toward creating shapes to be used as custom brushes (**Figure 14.11**). Here are a few tips:

▶ **Video Project**
03-08 *Custom Brushes*

- Reshape an oval object to create interesting shapes.

- Try to place a smaller object with a different fill color on top of your brush shape.

- Apply an effect (try Effects > Distort & Transform > Pucker & Bloat) to the object.

- Scale the object(s) down—it's better to create small brushes that can be enlarged by increasing an object's stroke width.

Figure 14.11 Six different shapes were created, then used to create custom art brushes that are available on the Brushes panel.

Create the Brush

Select the object(s), then click the New Brush icon on the bottom of the Brushes panel. Select a brush type in the New Brush dialog box, then click OK. Choose options in the Brush Options dialog that opens next. Remember to select Tints from the Method menu (under Colorization) so you can apply the current stroke color as a tint to the brush. Paint with the new custom brushes (**Figure 14.12**).

▶ **Video Project**
03-09 *Sketch with Paintbrush*

Figure 14.12a Stem strokes created from two custom art brushes

Figure 14.12b Petal strokes created from two custom art brushes

Figure 14.12c Flower strokes created from a custom Scatter brush and from two custom art brushes

Save Custom Brushes as a Library

On the Brushes panel, click the Brush Libraries menu and select Save Brushes to save all the brushes (added from other libraries and custom brushes) to a user-defined library. Enter a name for the new library and keep the default location. These brushes can now be accessed from any open Illustrator document by selecting User Defined from the Brush Libraries menu.

Use the Blob Brush

The Blob Brush is a dual-purpose brush. It lets you draw closed paths in a loose, freehand style, and it also lets you reshape existing closed paths, regardless of which tool created those paths. The Blob Brush can be used to produce the look of a sketch created with a traditional color marker.

Create an Object with the Blob Brush

 ACA Objective 3.9

TIP

Press the bracket keys ([or]) to decrease or increase the size of the brush tip for the Blob Brush tool.

Unlike the Paintbrush tool, which will create a stroked path, the Blob Brush tool will create a filled object. To create an object:

1   Choose the Blob Brush tool (Shift+B) 🖋.

2   Select a fill or stroke color.

3   Draw strokes to create a shape. Allow the strokes to crisscross or touch one another (**Figure 14.13**).

    When you release the mouse, a new, closed object is created and the Stroke color square will be set to the color selected in step 2.

Figure 14.13 The initial Blob Brush object. The Stroke square reflects the selected color automatically.

4 Without changing the stroke color, draw more strokes that intersect the shape you created (**Figure 14.14**). The new strokes are united with the existing shape automatically.

5 Select the Blob Brush object. The stroke color will automatically fill the shape (**Figure 14.15**).

The object will have a stroke of None and the Stroke color square will also be set to None.

Drag the Smooth tool along the edge of a selected Blob Brush object to reduce the number of points on the path.

Figure 14.14 More Blob Brush strokes were added to the object.

Figure 14.15 Selecting the final Blob Brush object shows that the object is a closed shape and contains a fill color only.

6 *Optional:* You can use the Blob Brush tool at any time to add to an existing object with a stroke of None. Just choose the same fill color. (Hint: Use the Eyedropper tool to sample the fill color).

That was pretty simple!

NOTE

Double-click the Blob Brush tool to open its Tool Options dialog box, where you can choose options and settings for the tool.

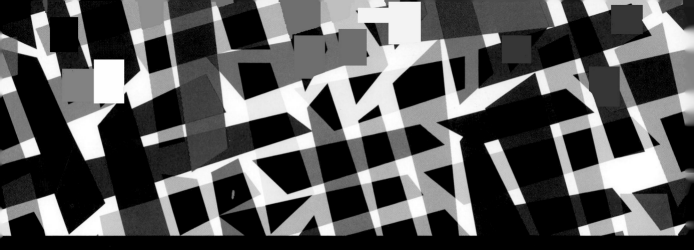

CHAPTER OBJECTIVES

Chapter Learning Objectives

- Create and style point type.
- Apply effects to type.
- Control text flow.
- Place type on a path.
- Create area type.
- Create outline type.

Chapter ACA Objectives

DOMAIN 4.0
CREATING DIGITAL GRAPHICS AND
ILLUSTRATIONS USING ADOBE ILLUSTRATOR CC

4.6 Add and manipulate type using Type tools.

CHAPTER 15

Type

In this chapter, you will learn how to work with type. Illustrator provides extensive controls for creating and styling type to enable you to transform it into a design element. You can create decorative type that functions as a graphic or a headline and create body type for reports, brochures, and product pieces.

You can also place type on the path (edge) of an object or within object shapes. Multiple lines of text can be threaded between text "rectangles" in a layout for a design project. Type can even be converted into a standard Illustrator object and completely reshaped. The graphic possibilities for creating, placing, and styling type in Illustrator are endless.

NOTE

This chapter supports the project created in Video Project 04. Go to the Video Project 04 page in the book's Web Edition to watch the entire project from beginning to end.

★ *ACA Objective 4.6*

▶ *Video Project 04-00 Introduction to Type*

Create Point Type

Point type stands by itself and is not associated with any drawn path or object. It can be composed of just one character or a group of several words, and it is most suitable for headlines, titles, or labels for web buttons.

▶ *Video Project 04-01 Creating Point Type*

To create point type (**Figure 15.1**):

1. Display the Character panel by choosing Window > Type > Character.
2. Choose View > Show Bounding Box.
3. Select the Type tool (T) $\mathbf{T}$. Click a blank area of an artboard. A flashing text insertion point appears.
4. Do either of the following:
    - On the Control panel, select a point size from the Font Size menu.
    - On the Character panel, select a point size from the Font Size menu.

5   Select a fill color and a stroke of None.

6   Enter some type. To complete the type object, do either of the following:

- Press Esc to automatically switch to the Selection tool.

- Command-click (Mac OS) or Ctrl-click (Windows) the artboard to deselect the type object while keeping the Type tool selected.

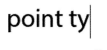 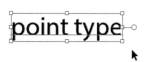

Figure 15.1 Creating and selecting a type object

Style Point Type

After entering type, you can use the Character, Color, Swatches, or Appearance panel to apply different styles (fonts, size, spacing), color, or effects to a selected type object. The type will remain editable (characters can be added or removed) after any of these edits.

To style point type:

1   Select the point type by clicking on it using either selection tool.

2   To resize the type, do either of the following:

- On the Character panel, change the Font Size value or choose a preset size from the menu.

- To manually resize type, drag a corner handle on the object's bounding box. Shift-drag a corner handle to resize proportionately (**Figure 15.2**).

- Drag a side handle to change either the horizontal or vertical scale.

    NOTE *Horizontal and vertical scale can also be modified by changing the values in those respective fields on the Character panel.*

Figure 15.2 Type dragged and resized, before (left) and after (right)

3 To change the font, click the Font Family menu arrow to display the list of available fonts in your system.

4 Roll over a font listing, then press the Up Arrow or Down Arrow key to preview different font families on the selected type. Press Return (Mac OS) or Enter (Windows) to apply the highlighted font (**Figure 15.3**).

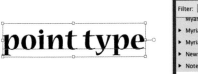

Figure 15.3 Choosing a font in the Font Family menu

You can also click the Font Family field (to highlight the current font name), then start typing a font name to display a temporary menu listing the fonts that closely match your entry. Press the Up Arrow or Down Arrow key to preview each font on your type, then press Return (Mac OS) or Enter (Windows) to apply the highlighted font.

5 To change the font style (weight or slant of the character face), choose a listing from the Font Style menu.

6 To modify the spacing between all the characters in the type object, change the value in the Tracking field, choose a preset value from the menu, or hold down Command-Option (Mac OS) or Ctrl-Alt (Windows) and press the Right Arrow or Left Arrow key. Positive values increase (loosen) the spacing; negative values reduce (tighten) the spacing (**Figure 15.4**).

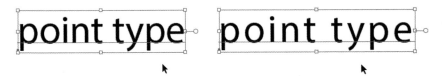

Figure 15.4 Changing font tracking

7 To modify the spacing between two characters, click with the Type tool between two characters, then change the value in the Kerning field or hold down Option (Mac OS) or Alt (Windows) and press the Right Arrow or Left Arrow key. Positive values increase the spacing; negative values reduce the spacing (**Figure 15.5**).

Figure 15.5 Changing type kerning

Style a Single Character or Word

You can give a single character or word in a type object its own styling and its own fill and stroke color. Even with these edits applied, you can still edit the text in the object.

Select the Type tool (T), then click within a type object. Drag across a character to select it; drag across or double-click a word to select it.

To modify the selected type, on the Character panel, change the font family, font style, font size, vertical or horizontal scale, baseline shift, or character rotation setting.

The most interactive and fun way to modify one character is to click the Touch Type tool on the Character panel, then click a character in a type object. A selection border will display around the character (**Figure 15.6**).

To scale proportionately, drag the upper-right handle. To scale horizontally, drag the lower-right handle. To scale vertically, drag the upper-left handle. To rotate, drag the little circle above the border. To move slightly, drag inside the selection border. While the character is selected, you can also change its fill and stroke color.

TIP

You can also apply a different fill and stroke color (and stroke width) to the selected type.

TIP

The Touch Type tool is grouped with the Type tool on the Tools panel as well. Click and hold on the Type tool to display the hidden tools and select the Touch Type tool.

Figure 15.6 Modifying a single character in a type object

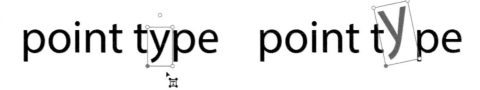

Apply Effects to Type

You can apply an effect from the Effect menu or from the Add New Effect menu on the Appearance panel to a selected type object (**Figure 15.7**).

Try the 3D > Extrude & Bevel, Distort & Transform submenu effects (use low values) or the Stylize > Drop Shadow or Scribble effects. The type will remain editable and settings on the Character panel (including font family and font style) can still be modified.

An effect can be removed at any time via the Appearance panel.

Figure 15.7 Adding an effect from the Appearance panel

Control Text Flow

When a design requires multiple lines or paragraphs of text, you can define the size and placement of one or more text rectangles to hold the text. Better still, you can link text rectangles and thread (flow) the text from one rectangle to the next. If you want to enter the text yourself, follow these steps. If you want to import a text file, see the sidebar "Import Text."

▶ *Video Project*
04-02 *Working with Text Flow and Text Wrap*

1 Create a new top-level layer on the Layers panel.

2 Select the Type tool (T). Select a font family, font style, and font size from the Control panel.

3 Drag to create a text rectangle. When you release the mouse, a flashing text insertion point appears.

4 Enter type. The type will wrap automatically to fit within the rectangle. Press Return (Mac OS) or Enter (Windows) if you need to start a new paragraph (**Figure 15.8**).

5 When you are finished typing, press Esc to switch to the Selection tool.

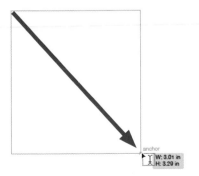

Here is our first try at area type. We are trying to show threading in Ai. You can enter type yourself or place a text file. Either way, your text will be placed in a text box rectangle.

Figure 15.8 Create a text rectangle (left) and the text you type in it wraps automatically (right).

IMPORT TEXT

Instead of typing large amounts of text, you can import text into your Illustrator document.

The simplest way to import text is to open a file in Microsoft Word, then copy all the text. In Illustrator, select the Type tool, drag to define a text rectangle, then choose Edit > Paste.

Another way to import text is to choose File > Place. In the Place dialog box, locate and select the text file to be imported, then click Place. A Microsoft Word Options or Text Import Options dialog box will open. Select options, then click OK.

The loaded text pointer ▦ appears. Drag to define a text rectangle. The text will display within the shape.

Thread Overflowing Text

If you import or enter more text than can fit into the text rectangle, then only some of the lines of text will be visible and a type overflow icon ⊞ will display near the lower-right corner of the text rectangle. The overflow icon signifies that there is overflow (hidden) text. Use either of the following tasks to make overflow text visible.

HANDLE A SMALL TEXT OVERFLOW

If you know that only a small amount text is overflowing, do this:

1   Using the Selection tool ▸, click the type to select its object.

2   Do any of the following:

- Drag a corner or side point on the text rectangle to enlarge the object and reveal the overflow text.

- Double-click the handle at the bottom center of the text rectangle to lengthen the rectangle automatically and reveal overflow text (**Figure 15.9**).

- Double-click the text to select the Type tool and display the text insertion point in the text. Choose Select > All to select all the text, then decrease the font size to reveal overflow text.

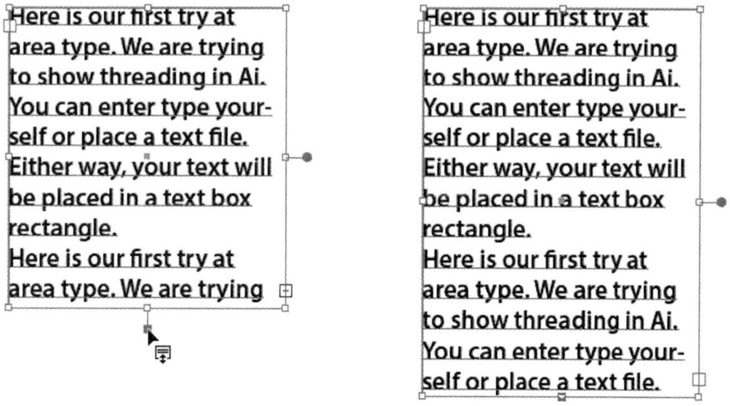

Here is our first try at area type. We are trying to show threading in Ai. You can enter type your-self or place a text file. Either way, your text will be placed in a text box rectangle. Here is our first try at area type. We are trying

Here is our first try at area type. We are trying to show threading in Ai. You can enter type your-self or place a text file. Either way, your text will be placed in a text box rectangle. Here is our first try at area type. We are trying to show threading in Ai. You can enter type your-self or place a text file.

Figure 15.9 Text box lengthened

HANDLE A LARGE TEXT OVERFLOW

If you know that there is a lot of overflow text, do this:

1 Using the Selection tool ▶, click the overflow icon in the out port (or click the text) to select the object.

2 Click the overflow icon again. The pointer becomes a loaded text icon (**Figure 15.10**).

3 Drag to create a new text rectangle to contain the overflow text or click to create a duplicate of the current text rectangle.

The two text rectangles are linked automatically and overflow text flows into the new object (**Figure 15.11**).

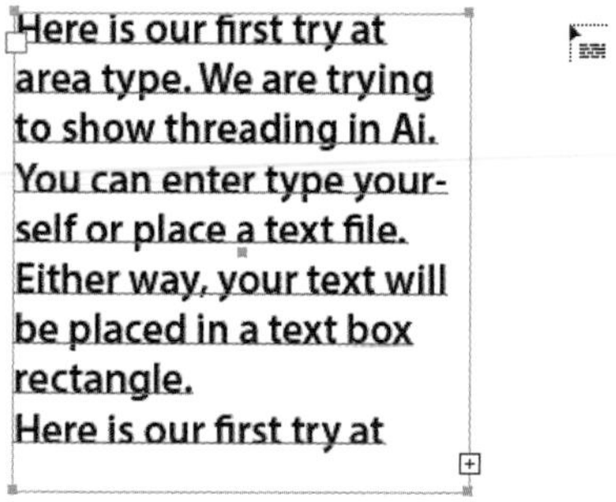

Here is our first try at area type. We are trying to show threading in Ai. You can enter type your-self or place a text file. Either way, your text will be placed in a text box rectangle. Here is our first try at

Here is our first try at area type. We are trying to show threading in Ai. You can enter type your-self or place a text file. Either way, your text will be placed in a text box rectangle. Here is our first try at

area type. We are trying to show threading in Ai. You can enter type yourself or place a text file.

Figure 15.10 The loaded text icon

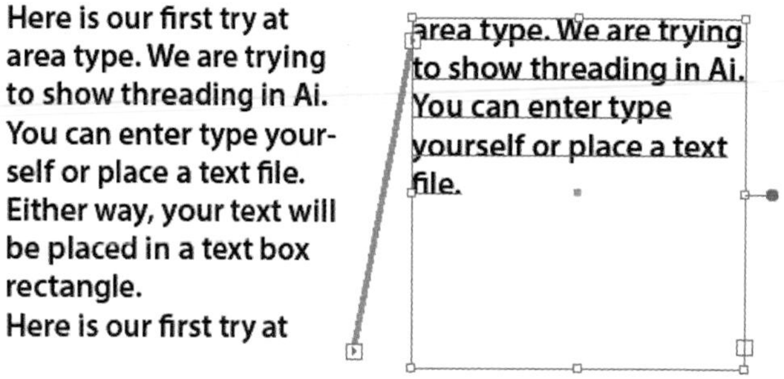

Figure 15.11 Overflow text flows into the new rectangle.

Wrap Text Around Art

When an art object is placed in front of a text rectangle, the Text Wrap command can be used to force the text to wrap around the graphic.

To wrap text around art:

1 Position an art object or symbol in front of the text rectangle.

2 Select both objects, then choose Object > Text Wrap > Make.

   Text in the rectangle flows around the art object's edge (**Figure 15.12**).

TIP

The art object can be repositioned or scaled at any time and the text will rewrap around it automatically.

3 To adjust the distance between the edge of the art object and the text, choose Object > Text Wrap > Text Wrap Options.

4 In the Text Wrap Options dialog box, select Preview, then increase the Offset value to increase the space around the art object. Press Tab to preview any new values. Click OK.

In amet perfecto forensibus sed, eu his agam deterruisset, vix everti delicata dissentiunt ad. Vel cu partem delicata, his nobis tibique platonem te, te viderer prodesset vituperata ius. Eripuit suscipiantur no sed, ludico commune ea mea. Vix ne oporteat aliquando deterruisset. Ex sea adhuc adolescens, eu vis scaevola moderatius, ei soluta senserit nec.

Pri mollis euismod noluisse ut. Ei scripta dignissim pro, pericula te eam, sea ad ludico inermis laborapostulant mei ea, usu nominati atomo- Erant discere labores mei cu. Lorem amet, rebum epicurei corrumpit te inimicus conveni- soluta vel, eu vim evertitur. Has homero assueverit te. No quam voluptatum mel. lens usu, nonumy Possit dolorem cu vel, voluptatum, usu at

tibique luptatum mus. Liber detraxit rum sensibus ei. ipsum dolor sit ius, vel id porro re. Ex novum nullam dictas equidem minim tam- id sonet inso- ap- petere vix at. ad quo graeco bonorum dolorum.

Qui quas atqui altera labores id, viris pro. An congue dicant dignis- vel. Semper facilisi eum no, an duo tamquam ponderum, altera sensibus ex per. Ex pro modus munere verear.

nonumy ei. Mel legere modum consetetur in ad- sim id. El laborar us forensibus

Figure 15.12 Text wraps around an art object.

Place Type on a Path

▶ *Video Project 04-03* Placing Type on a Path or Inside an Area

You can place type along the edge of any path in your artwork, enabling you to flow your type around the graphic shapes in your artwork. How cool is that?

To place type on a path:

1 Select the Type On A Path tool. Note the path line indicator on the tool icon.

2 Click the path of an open (a line) or closed object. Any attributes (such as fill or stroke) on that object are removed and the text insertion point flashes on the edge of the path.

3 Enter type. It will follow along the edge of the path.

4 Press Esc to automatically switch to the Selection tool.

TIP

If you reshape a path, the text will conform to the new shape.

Reposition Type on a Path

Once placed on a path, the type can be repositioned along or flipped to the opposite side of the path.

To change the position of type on a path:

1 Using the Selection tool, click the type path's object.

Center, left, and right control brackets appear.

2 To reposition the type block, do any of the following:

- To move the type block along the path, drag the center bracket right or left (**Figure 15.13**).

- To reposition the starting point of the type on the path, drag the left bracket, which is near the start of the type (**Figure 15.14**).

NOTE *Be careful not to move the left bracket too far along the path, because this may cause type to overflow past the right bracket. If text overflows, the overflow icon will appear by the right bracket.*

Figure 15.13 Dragging the center bracket to move the type along the path

Figure 15.14 Moving the left bracket

- To flip the type to the opposite side of (or inside) the path, drag the center bracket across the path. Use this method to position type on the inside of a curved or circular path (**Figure 15.15**).

Figure 15.15 Flipping the type

Create Area Type

You're not limited to just placing type along the edge of a path shape. You can also place multiple lines of type inside a shape, so that the type will wrap within the edges (or area) of the shape. This is yet another way to graphically enhance your type.

To create area type:

1 Select the Area Type tool 🄣. Note the dashed circle indicator around the tool icon.

2 Click the edge of a closed object or an open object that has a concave area. Any attributes (such as fill or stroke) are removed and the text insertion point flashes inside the object.

3 Enter or copy and paste several lines of type. It will wrap within the object shape (**Figure 15.16**).

4 Press Esc to switch to the Selection tool.

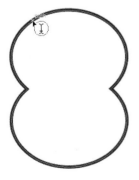

Figure 15.16 Adding area type to an object

Fit Area Type

Once inside an object, your type may need to be adjusted to create a better fit within the shape.

Using the Selection tool, click the type area's object, then do any of the following:

- On the Character panel, increase or decrease the font size.

- On the Paragraph panel, click the Align Center button at the top of the panel to center the type within the object. (The Align Center button is also accessible from the Control panel.)

- Choose Type > Area Type Options. In the Area Type Options dialog box, select Preview. Under Offset, increase the Insert Spacing value to add spacing between the type and the object edge (**Figure 15.17**).

TIP

After deselecting the area type object, remember to set type alignment back to the default setting by clicking the Align Left button on the Paragraph panel or Control panel.

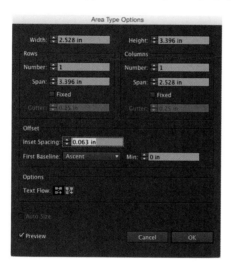

Figure 15.17 Adjusting area type for a better fit via the Area Type Options dialog box

NOTE

You can reshape or recolor an area type's object by selecting its path with the Direct Selection tool, then moving points or segments or applying a fill or stroke color.

Create Outline Type

When you are finished editing and styling type, you can convert the type into outlines (standard Illustrator objects). The converted "graphic" objects will no longer be editable type, but the character's paths can be reshaped and transformed using all the editing techniques you have already learned. This works best with large type sizes used for display type.

1. Create a large point type object, then choose Type > Create Outlines to convert the type to individual objects.

▶ *Video Project*
04-04 Using 3D Effects and Creating Type Outlines

▶ *Video Project*
04-05 Letter Shapes into Logos

▶ *Video Project*
04-06 Using Type and Shapes in a Logo

2   Using the Direct Selection tool, drag any point, segment, or direction handle to modify the shape of the path.

3   Reposition or transform any of the objects and apply a different fill or stroke color to some or all of the objects (**Figure 15.18**).

Figure 15.18 Type turned into outlines to become individual Illustrator objects, which were then individually transformed

OUTLINES   OUTLINES

Flow Type on a Circle

▶ *Video Project 04-07* Placing Type on a Circular Path

▶ *Video Project 04-08* Creating a Story Layout Using Type and Graphics

Placing upward-reading type on the top and bottom of a circular path is a classic illustration task that all designers would do well to learn. The key step in this task is to cut the circular path to create two separate upper and lower semi-circular objects to enable each path's type block to be repositioned and shifted independently.

To position type on a circle:

1   Create a circle, then use the Scissors tool ✂ to cut two opposite anchor points on the path.

2   Using the Type On A Path tool ↘, enter type first on the upper semi-circular object, then on the lower semi-circular object (**Figure 15.19**).

Figure 15.19 Type on a path entered on two semi-circular objects

3   Adjust the position of the type on each selected path object by dragging their respective center brackets. Use the Baseline Shift option on the Character panel to shift the type above or below its path.

4   Place other objects in front or behind the type objects to enhance the logo (**Figure 15.20**).

Figure 15.20 A logo created with type-on-a-circle text

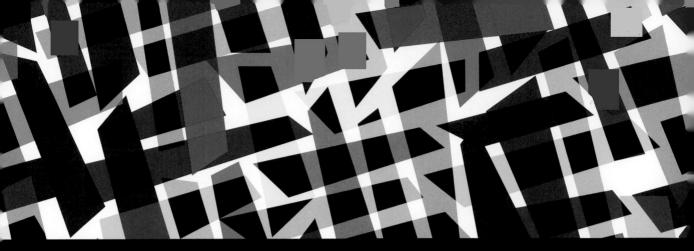

CHAPTER OBJECTIVES

Chapter Learning Objectives

- Place an image as an embedded object.
- Place an image as a linked object.
- Create a clipping mask.
- Work with Image Trace.
- Use transformations to fit an object into a 3D drawing.
- Use the perspective tools to create a perspective drawing.

Chapter ACA Objectives

DOMAIN 3.0
UNDERSTANDING ADOBE ILLUSTRATOR CC

3.5 Demonstrate knowledge of layers and masks.

3.8 Demonstrate knowledge of how and why illustrators employ different views and modes throughout the course of a project, including vector/outline vs. display/ appearance, isolate mode, and various Draw modes.

DOMAIN 4.0
CREATING DIGITAL GRAPHICS AND ILLUSTRATIONS USING ADOBE ILLUSTRATOR CC

4.3 Transform graphics and illustrations.

4.5 Import assets into a project.

4.7 Create digital graphics and illustrations using 3D and perspective tools in Illustrator.

CHAPTER 16

Advanced Drawing

Illustrator isn't limited to working with vector objects only. Bitmap images can be incorporated into your artwork as imagery that is placed either next to or behind vector objects or that is used as a fill within an object.

In this chapter, you will learn how to bring bitmap images into your artwork and place them as an embedded or linked object. You will also learn how to create clipping masks that can be used to hide portions of vector objects or bitmap images. In addition, you will learn how to trace a placed bitmap image to automatically convert it into vector objects that will output as paths with sharp, crisp edges.

Finally, you will learn how to fit an object onto shapes in a perspective drawing and how to attach art and text objects onto the sides of a perspective grid.

NOTE

This chapter supports the project created in Video Project 05. Go to the Video Project 05 page in the book's Web Edition to watch the entire project from beginning to end.

Place Bitmap Images as Embedded Objects

★ *ACA Objective 4.5*

Illustrator enables you to bring in bitmap images that were created using a digital camera or created in a bitmap editing application such as Photoshop. The bitmap image will be **embedded** in your document as a non-vector object. You can import a bitmap image using the default Place command settings or you can display an Import Options dialog box to customize how the image is imported.

▶ *Video Project 05-01 Placing Embedded Images*

Figure 16.1 The loaded graphics icon displaying one of four images

To place an embedded image:

1   Choose File > Place. In the Place dialog box, locate and select one or more images.

2   Deselect Link at the bottom of the dialog box.

3   If the image is from Photoshop and contains multiple layers, select Show Import Options. Click Place.

4   In the Photoshop Import Options dialog box, do either of the following:

   ▪ Click Convert Layers To Objects to preserve each layer as a nested object within a group on the Layers panel. Transparency values are listed as editable appearances on the Appearance panel. Blending modes that are also available in Illustrator are preserved and remain editable. (For a list of blending modes in Illustrator, view the Blending Modes menu on the Transparency panel.)

   ▪ Click Flatten Layers To A Single Image to create a flattened version of the file.

5   Click OK.

   The loaded graphics icon appears (**Figure 16.1**). The icon displays a thumbnail of the first loaded image and lists the total number of loaded images.

6   Press the Left Arrow or Right Arrow key to cycle through the thumbnails on the loaded graphics icon. Drag to place an image. Drag again to place the next loaded image.

Place Bitmap Images as Links

You can also choose to place a linked (rather than embedded) image into your document. Illustrator places a screen version of the image (with an X across it) to serve as a placeholder and maintains a link to the external source file.

> **NOTE** *There are advantages to using the link feature: It keeps your document file size small (as no pixel data is stored in the file), and it enables you or someone else to edit the source file outside of Illustrator and have those edits update in the linked image.*

To place a linked image, choose File > Place. In the Place dialog box, locate and select one or more images. Select Link at the bottom of the dialog box, then click Place. The loaded graphics icon will appear. Drag to place an image.

Manage Linked Images

You can use commands on the Links or Control panel to manage your placed linked images.

Use the Links Panel

The Links panel lists the linked or embedded images currently in your document. An embedded image displays the embedded icon 🖼. A linked image displays its filename; double-click a linked image listing to expand the panel and display link information.

The Links panel provides controls for managing linked images (**Figure 16.2**). The icons along the bottom of the panel enable you to:

Figure 16.2 The Links panel

- Relink From Creative Cloud Libraries (for an image that was placed by dragging it from Illustrator's Libraries panel)
- Relink (to relocate the image using the Place dialog box)
- Go To Link (to locate the image in your document)
- Update Link (when a source image has been modified outside of Illustrator)
- Edit Original (to edit the source file)

The Links panel will display alert icons to indicate that a linked image is either missing ⊗ or has been modified ⚠. You can use the Relink or Update Link icons to resolve these issues.

Use the Control Panel

The left side of the Control panel displays the name of a selected linked image, its color mode, and its ppi value (image resolution).

The Control panel (**Figure 16.3**) also enables you to manage a linked image by providing access to the same controls found on the Links panel:

- Click the linked image filename to display a menu containing the same options as found on the Links panel.
- Click Embed to embed the selected linked image and break the link to the source file.

Figure 16.3 Linked image options on the Control panel

Linked File   face.psd **Transparent CMYK**   PPI: 300   Embed   Edit Original   Image Trace ▾   Mask   Opacity: 100%

- Click Edit Original to open the source file for the linked image in its original application. Edit, save, and close the source file, then return to Illustrator. An alert dialog box will ask if you want to update the modified linked image. Click Yes.

★ *ACA Objective 3.5*

Create a Clipping Mask

▶ *Video Project*
05-03 Creating a
Clipping Mask

When objects are part of a **clipping mask**, the topmost object crops (masks) the objects that are below it. Portions of the lower objects that fall within the path of the topmost object remain visible, while portions that extend beyond its path are hidden and don't print. The clipping object and the objects being masked are also referred to as a "clipping set."

To create a clipping mask:

1 Arrange one or more objects to be masked on an artboard. Stack the object that will become the mask in front of the other objects (**Figure 16.4**). Select all of the objects.

2 Choose Object > Clipping Mask > Make. The objects will be masked by the topmost object (**Figure 16.5**).

On the Layers panel, a new Clip Group appears that contains the objects in the clipping mask. The topmost object in the group will be converted into a Clipping Path and be listed as such on the Layers panel.

Figure 16.4 The elements arranged and stacked for a clipping mask

Figure 16.5 The clipping mask result

Draw Inside mode offers a different method for clipping imagery. You create a clipping object first, then draw or paste other objects inside it.

1 Using the Selection tool, select an object to become the clipping object. On the lower part of the Tools panel, click the Draw Inside button  to activate that drawing mode. A dashed border appears around the corners of the selected object to designate it as a clipping object.

2 Draw shapes over the selected object. (Objects drawn beyond the edge of the clipping object will be totally hidden.) Choose Edit > Copy to copy an object or a placed image, then choose Edit > Paste.

3 To return to Draw Normal mode, double-click the artboard with a selection tool or press Shift+D. The dashed border disappears.

Edit the Contents of a Clipping Mask

The objects within a clipping mask can be repositioned, restacked, and edited at any time and still remain masked.

To edit the contents of a clipping mask:

- Using the Selection tool, select a clipping mask. On the Control panel, click the Edit Contents icon ◈ .

- Double-click one of the selected objects to enter isolation mode. Edit the object. Click other objects to edit them (**Figure 16.6**). When you are finished editing, double-click the artboard to exit isolation mode.

TIP

Instead of using the Edit Contents and isolation mode method, you can use the Direct Selection tool to select and edit any object in a clipping mask.

Figure 16.6 Editing the contents of the clipping mask

- To add an object to a clipping mask, draw or reposition it in front of clipping mask, then drag its listing into the Clip Group on the Layers panel. Its position in the Clip Group stack on the Layers panel will determine its stacking position among the objects in the clipping mask.

Release a Clipping Mask

You can release a clipping mask and remove the clipping effect at any time. This feature applies to a clipping mask created via the Object > Clipping Mask command or via Draw Inside mode.

Select a clipping mask using the Selection tool. Choose Object > Clipping Mask > Release. The masked objects will become completely visible and the clipping path object will lose its stroke and fill. (You can locate and select the former clipping path via its listing on the Layers panel or by using Smart Guides.)

★ *ACA Objective 4.5*

Use Image Trace

▶ *Video Project 05-02 Using Image Trace*

The Image Trace feature enables you to convert a bitmap image into editable vector art composed of shaped paths with colored fills. You can use options on the Image Trace panel to generate a close simulation of the shapes and colors in the image or generate a simplified version composed of a limited set of colors, shades, or just line work.

NOTE *Designers also use Image Trace to quickly convert a bitmap image of a logo into vector paths to produce artwork that will output as clean, sharp lines and edges.*

Figure 16.7 The Image Trace panel

You can apply Image Trace to a linked or embedded image that you've placed into your document. Use the Image Trace panel to access all the options for this feature.

To trace an image:

1 Select a placed image. Choose Window > Image Trace to display the panel (**Figure 16.7**).

2 Click one of the six tracing preset icons along the top of the panel or select an option from the Preset menu. A series of progress bars will appear and a tracing will be generated (**Figures 16.8**, **16.9**, and **16.10**).

NOTE

The Control panel also provides access to some of the essential options found on the Image Trace panel.

Figure 16.8 The original placed image

Figure 16.9 A 16-color trace

Figure 16.10 A 4-color trace

3   From the View menu on the Image Trace panel, select an option to view the resulting paths. The default setting is Tracing Results.

NOTE

A traced image is "live," meaning that you can reselect the object and modify the Image Trace panel settings to generate a different trace result.

Expand a Tracing

When you are satisfied with the tracing results, you can convert it to standard paths, which can then be selected and recolored, reshaped, or edited as with any other object in Illustrator. Once expanded, the trace can no longer be modified via the Image Trace panel.

To expand a tracing, select a tracing object, then click Expand on the Control panel. The former Layers panel listing of Image Tracing will be converted into a Group listing, with the path objects nested within the group.

★ *ACA Objective 4.3*

▶ *Video Project 05-05* Applying a Logo to a Perspective Drawing—Part 1

Fit an Object into a 3D and Perspective Drawing

▶ *Video Project 05-06* Applying a Logo to a Perspective Drawing—Part 2

As a designer and illustrator, you may need to create artwork that incorporates perspective drawing. This might involve creating a perspective drawing from scratch or placing artwork into an existing perspective drawing. In the following section, you will look at four methods for fitting a logo into a perspective drawing.

Use the Shear Tool

Experiment with the Shear tool (on the Scale tool hidden tool menu) to flatten an object to match the angles of a larger shape in a perspective drawing.

Select an object or group, then select the Shear tool. By default, the point of origin for the tool is set to the center of the selection. Slowly drag downward and to the right to flatten and distort the selection to match the angles of the larger shape (**Figure 16.11**).

Figure 16.11 The logo flattened and distorted with the Shear tool

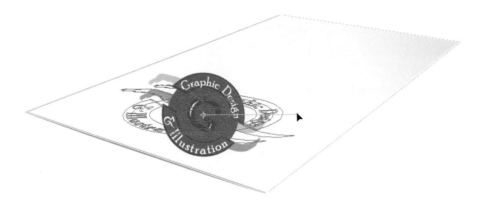

Envelope Distort

Next, you'll experiment with Envelope Distort. Using the Pen tool, click to create a closed path that matches the larger shape. Select both the new path and your artwork object. Then choose Object > Envelope Distort > Make With Top Object to fit the object into the Pen tool path (**Figure 16.12**).

Figure 16.12 The logo fitted into a Pen tool path with Envelope Distort

Art Brush

Experiment with applying a logo as an art brush. Select the logo object or group. Click New Brush on the Brushes panel and select Art Brush to convert the object into an art brush. Use the Paintbrush tool to draw a stroke with the new art brush across a curved shape in the drawing.

3D Mapping

★ *ACA Objective 4.7*

To experiment with 3D mapping, drag the artwork logo that you want to fit onto a 3D shape into the Symbols panel to create a new symbol. To create a sphere, draw a curved path shape, apply a white stroke, then choose Effect > 3D > Revolve. In the 3D Revolve Options dialog box, under Revolve, select From: Left Edge, then click Map Art. In the Map Art dialog box, select your new symbol from the Symbol menu. Drag the symbol in the light/shadow preview to position it on the sphere (**Figure 16.13**). Click OK twice.

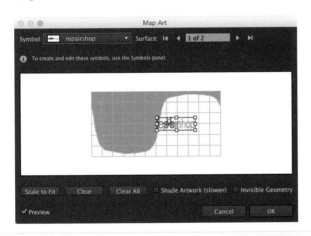

Figure 16.13 Positioning the symbol on the sphere object via the Map Art dialog box

Use Perspective Grid Feature

★ *ACA Objective 4.7*

 ▶ *Video Project 05-07* Logos on Perspective Grid

For the ultimate in perspective drawing, Illustrator provides the Perspective Grid tool to enable you to quickly generate a one-point or two-point, nonprinting perspective grid. You can attach existing objects to any of the planes on the grid. Objects on the grid can still be edited.

Before you draw the perspective grid, create the objects you want to place in perspective.

Draw a Two-Point Grid

TIP

To choose between a one-point and two-point grid, choose an option from the View > Perspective Grid submenu.

To create a two-point grid, select the Perspective Grid tool. The perspective grid appears on the current artboard. A Plane switching widget also appears in the upper-left corner of the document window.

Attach Objects to the Perspective Grid

TIP

If you need to draw a new object for your perspective design, choose View > Perspective Grid > Hide Grid. Draw the object, then show the grid again.

Once the perspective grid is created, you can attach objects to it. To do this, select the Perspective Selection tool, click a plane on the Plane switching widget, then drag an existing object onto that side of the grid (**Figure 16.14**). Click the bottom plane on the Plane switching widget to place an object on the ground plane in the drawing.

Once on the plane, you can drag to move the object, scale it using the selection handles, or recolor it using any of Illustrator's color editing panels (**Figure 16.15**).

Figure 16.14 Click a plane on the Plane switching widget, then drag an object onto that plane.

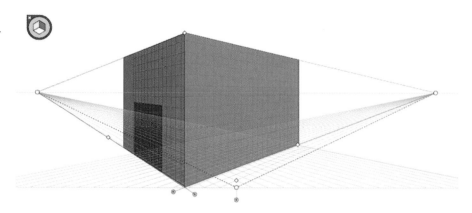

Figure 16.15 Logo objects placed in front of the wall objects

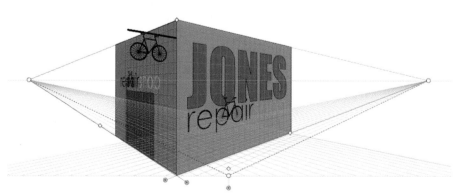

TIP

Shapes can also be drawn directly on the grid. Choose either perspective tool, click a plane on the Plane switching widget, then select a shape tool and draw a shape on the grid.

Create an Interior Using Perspective

With the Perspective Grid feature, you're not limited to placing objects on the outside of a three-dimensional shape; you can also place objects on the inside of a three-dimensional shape. With a one-point perspective grid, you can create a drawing of a room interior complete with windows, flooring, and furniture (**Figures 16.16** and **16.17**).

▶ *Video Project*
05-08 *Constructing*
an Interior Using
Perspective—Part 1

▶ *Video Project*
05-09 *Constructing*
an Interior Using
Perspective—Part 2

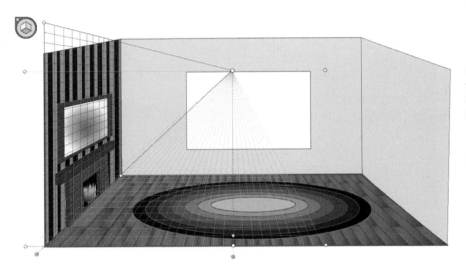

Figure 16.16 The basic wall and floor shapes applied to the one-point perspective grid

▶ *Video Project*
05-10 *Constructing*
an Interior Using
Perspective—Part 3

Figure 16.17 The finished room interior drawn using the perspective grid

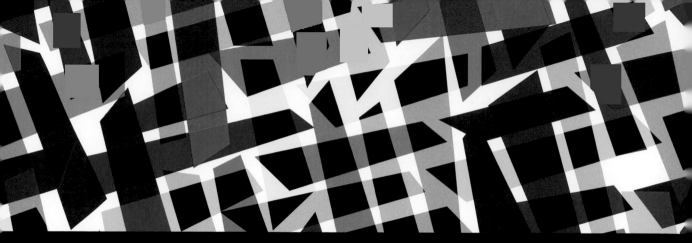

CHAPTER OBJECTIVES

Chapter Learning Objectives

- Prepare artwork for output.
- Learn about Separations Preview.
- Learn about Pixel Preview.
- Output to print.
- Export to web formats.
- Place vector artwork in Adobe Photoshop.

Chapter ACA Objectives

DOMAIN 2.0
UNDERSTANDING DIGITAL GRAPHICS AND
ILLUSTRATIONS

2.5 Demonstrate knowledge of image
resolution, image size, and image file
format for web, video, and print.

DOMAIN 5.0
ARCHIVE, EXPORT, AND PUBLISH GRAPHICS USING
ADOBE ILLUSTRATOR CC

5.1 Prepare images for web, print, and video.

5.2 Export digital graphics and illustrations to
various file formats.

CHAPTER 17

Output

Now that you have created various artwork pieces in Illustrator, it's time to focus on outputting high-quality files, whether it be for print or web. Preparing an artwork file for its destination format requires performing a number of tasks.

For print, these tasks involve confirming that colors are defined correctly as process or spot, previewing color separations, and specifying appropriate settings in the Print dialog box. For web and screen, these tasks involve specifying the correct color mode, and aligning object paths to the pixel grid. Both types of output require choosing a resolution for certain effects that will be rasterized when the artwork is exported.

In this chapter, you will learn how to work with spot colors for print, how to work with the Separations Preview panel, what the essential settings are in the Print dialog box, and how to export an Illustrator file to the JPEG, PNG, and SVG formats. Finally, you will find out how to bring artwork into Adobe Photoshop.

NOTE

This chapter supports the project created in Video Project 05. Go to the Video Project 05 page in the book's Web Edition to watch the entire project from beginning to end.

Prepare Artwork for Print Output

In a lot of computer applications, sending a file to print is a simple procedure. In Illustrator, getting the high-quality graphics to output satisfactorily requires more work. In this section, we will review some of the features that can help take the guesswork out of obtaining quality print output.

Keep in mind that Illustrator vector objects are resolution-independent. They will print at the resolution of the printing device. The higher the device resolution, the higher the edge quality of shapes in the printed image.

Document Color Mode

When you're preparing a file for print, you first need to know what type of printer will be used.

COMMERCIAL PRESS: CMYK COLOR

NOTE

The printing term sepa-rations denotes the process of separating color in the artwork to one of the four CMYK printing plates.

A commercial press prints colors in the artwork as **process colors** which are a com-bination of the four CMYK ink colors. Each ink color is printed separately onto a roll of paper using one of four color plates—a Cyan, Magenta, Yellow, and Black plate. For this type of printer, make sure the File > Document Color Mode submenu is set to CMYK Color. Commercial printing is used when dozens (if not hundreds) of copies of the file are needed.

COMPOSITE COLOR PRINTER: RGB COLOR

A composite color printer prints all the colors together directly on a single sheet of paper. For this type of printer, make sure the File > Document Color Mode submenu is set to RGB Color. The printer will convert the Illustrator file from RGB Color mode to CMYK Color mode and will produce a print using the four CMYK color inks. Use composite printers when you need only one copy (or a few) of the file.

Artboard Size

Here are some guidelines for artboard size in regard to print output.

- When printing to a composite printer, make sure the size of each artboard is less than or equal to the size of the printer media (the paper).

- When printing to a commercial printer, make sure the size of each artboard is less than the size of the printer media so that any **printer's marks** will display (see the "Print Dialog Box Settings" section later in this chapter). Ask a representative at the print shop for the media dimensions.

- If you need to scale the artboard and artwork down to fit the print media, see the information about the Scaling menu in the "Print Dialog Box Settings" section later in this chapter.

Bleed

For either printer type, make sure objects that need to print right to the edge of the paper extend off the edge of the artboard slightly. The part of an object that is beyond the edge is referred to as a bleed.

Spot Color

Occasionally, a client will specify that a shape or logo in a design needs to be printed with a specific premixed color. This is referred to as a spot color. A spot color prints on its own plate, in addition to the four CMYK process color plates.

To define a color as a spot color in Illustrator:

1 Ask your client to specify a color-matching system name or brand (such as PANTONE) and a spot color number from that system.

2 On the bottom of the Swatches panel, click the Swatch Libraries menu. From the Color Books submenu, select the specified color-matching system.

3 In the color book library that opens, enter the specified spot color number in the search field at the top. The matching spot color swatch will display on the panel (**Figure 17.1**).

4 Click the swatch to copy it to the Swatches panel.

NOTE

On the Swatches panel, a spot color is designated by a small black dot in the lower-right corner of its swatch.

Figure 17.1 Search a color book library for a spot color.

5   Apply the spot color swatch to the artwork object.

While the object is selected, the Color panel (**Figure 17.2**) will display the spot color name and number. A Tint slider enables you to adjust the color intensity (the amount of ink applied) of the printed color.

Figure 17.2 A spot color displayed on the Color panel

Separations Preview Panel

The Separations Preview panel lets you preview how the C, M, Y, and K inks will print artwork color on the individual printing plates in commercial printing.

1   With a CMYK Color mode document open, choose Window > Separations Preview to display the panel.

2   At the top of the Separations Preview panel, select Overprint Preview. The four separation inks (Cyan, Magenta, Yellow, and Black) and any spot color inks being used in the artwork become enabled on the panel.

3   To hide one of the four separation inks, click its eye icon. Cutout areas shown in white designate where the hidden ink will print at 100% and show that no other inks will print in those areas (**Figure 17.3**).

Figure 17.3 Hiding the Black separation ink reveals the white cutout areas where black will print at 100%.

4 To view a single separation ink, Option-click (Mac OS) or Alt-click (Windows) an eye icon on the panel. All other separation inks will be hidden. In this case, white cutout areas designate where the selected ink will *not* print. Option-click (Mac OS) or Alt-click (Windows) the eye icon again to display all separation inks.

5 Click a spot color eye icon to hide its separation ink (**Figure 17.4**). The preview will show white cutout areas where the color was applied—confirming that only the spot color ink (and not the other inks) will print in those areas.

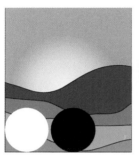

Figure 17.4 Hiding the spot color separation ink revealed the white cutout area where the spot color will print.

Resolution for Rasterized Effects

★ *ACA Objective 2.5*

Raster (bitmapped) effects are effects that will be applied as pixels and not as vector shapes. Raster effects include SVG filters; Drop Shadow, Inner and Outer Glows, and the Feather commands from the Effect > Stylize submenu along with all Photoshop Effects listed in the Effect menu.

To determine the resolution that will be applied to raster effects:

1 Choose Effect > Document Raster Effects Settings.

2 In the Document Raster Effects Settings dialog box, select High (300 ppi) [pixels per inch] from the Resolution menu (**Figure 17.5**).

3 Under Background, click Transparent.

4 Click OK. Settings will be applied to any raster effects in the document.

> **NOTE** *The resolution setting for raster effects is not permanent and can be changed at any time. Changing this setting will cause raster effects to be recalculated, but you will see little or no change in their appearance.*

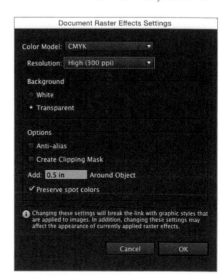

Figure 17.5 The Document Raster Effects Settings dialog box

Print Dialog Box Settings

Now that the file is ready for printing, it's time to look at some of the essential settings in the Print dialog box.

To print a document on a color printer directly from Illustrator:

1 Choose File > Print to open the Print dialog box.

2 From the Printer menu, select a composite color or commercial separations-capable printer that is available in your system.

3 In the options list at the left, click General to display that panel (**Figure 17.6**).

Figure 17.6 The General panel in the Print dialog box

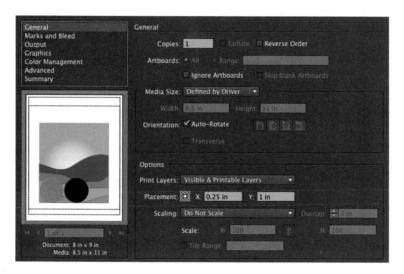

4 Under Artboards, click All or click Range and enter specific artboard numbers. Use the navigation arrows below the preview to view each artboard.

5 From the Media Size menu, select Defined by Driver.

6 Under Orientation, make sure Auto-Rotate is selected.

7 If you need to scale the artboards down to fit the print media, select Fit to Page from the Scaling menu. Leave all other options set to their defaults.

If you don't want to print the file right now, click Done to close the Print dialog box, then save your document to save the current print settings to the file.

8 If you're printing to a composite color printer, select Color Management in the options list at the left to display that panel. From the Printer Profile menu, select the recommended profile for the chosen composite printer. Click Print to close the dialog box and print the file, and proceed to the next tasks.

If you are creating separations for a commercial printer, continue with the remaining steps.

9 Select Marks and Bleed in the options list at the left to display that panel (**Figure 17.7**).

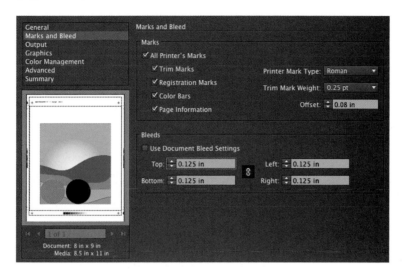

Figure 17.7 The Marks and Bleed panel in the Print dialog box

10 Under Marks, select All Printer's Marks.

11 Under Bleeds, deselect Use Document Bleed Settings, then enter values as specified by your print shop. Portions of objects that extend (or bleed) beyond the artboard edge will print in this added area.

12 Select the Output category in the options list at the left to display that panel (**Figure 17.8**). Note that changes in this panel are almost always done by the print shop and not by the graphic artist or designer.

NOTE

The Trim Marks option will place marks that indicate where to trim the page and cut off the bleed area.

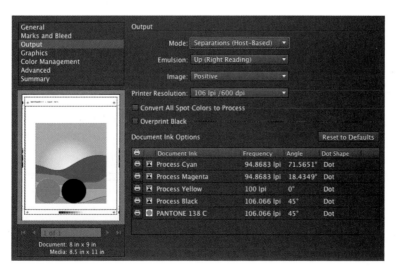

Figure 17.8 The Output panel in the Print dialog box

TIP

To convert a single spot color to process (and save the expense of one extra printing plate), in the Document Ink Options area, click its spot color icon ⬤ to change it to a process color icon.

13 From the Mode menu, select Separations (Host-Based); the Document Ink Options become available.

- If you or your client decide not to print spot colors to separate plates, select Convert All Spot Colors To Process.

- To allow black fills and strokes to print over the C, M, and Y separation inks (and not create cutout areas), select Overprint Black.

14 Click Print to close the dialog box and print the file.

TIP

To prevent a spot color from printing, click its print color icon 🖶.

Prepare Artwork for Web Output

Web and screen output have their own requirements that need to be addressed to ensure quality output.

Document Color Mode

NOTE

When you choose Web from the Profile menu in the New Document dialog box, the Color Mode is set to RGB automatically.

Web browsers and mobile screens display images in RGB color. Choose File > Document Color Mode > RGB Color to set the document to that mode.

Artboard Size

Select the Artboard tool to enter Artboard mode. Resize the artboards to match the pixel dimensions of the web pages you are exporting to. Ask your web developer for these dimensions.

Align to Pixel Grid

When an Illustrator file is exported to either the JPEG or PNG format, the artwork will be rasterized, meaning vector paths and shapes will be converted to pixels and lose their crisp, sharp edges.

To minimize blurring along edges, Illustrator provides the Align To Pixel Grid feature. This feature automatically positions any vertical and horizontal path segment on an object to align with the pixel grid, even if the object is moved or scaled. (Path segments that are not vertical or horizontal are not aligned.)

To align all future objects, do either of the following:

- For a new document, choose File > New to open the New Document dialog box. Select Web from the Profile menu. Align New Objects To Pixel Grid is selected automatically.

- In an existing document, on the Transform panel, select Align New Objects To Pixel Grid from the panel menu.

TIP

To align selected objects created before activating Align New Objects To Pixel Grid, select the Align To Pixel Grid option at the bottom of the Transform panel.

Pixel Preview

The Pixel Preview feature enables you to see how exported web artwork will appear. With either Align To Pixel Grid option active, choose View > Pixel Preview to preview the artwork as a 72 ppi (pixels per inch) bitmap image. Vertical and horizontal paths that are aligned to the grid will not appear blurry.

Resolution for Rasterized Effects

Since web and screen displays are often small devices with low-resolution output (compared to print output), a lower resolution setting can be applied to any raster effects.

The steps for using the Document Raster Effects Settings dialog box are the same as in the "Prepare Artwork for Print Output" section earlier in this chapter, except you would choose Screen (72 ppi) from the Resolution menu.

Export Artwork

Illustrator provides ways to export files to JPEG or PNG format (two of the most popular formats used for web imagery) and also to SVG format (a format gaining in popularity because it preserves vector paths and shapes in the exported graphics file).

★ *ACA Objective 5.2*

Export to JPEG or PNG Format

The JPEG and PNG file formats describe an image as a grid of pixels and generate a file that is compact, but set to a specific resolution.

To export artwork in JPEG or PNG format:

1 Choose File > Export.

2 In the Export dialog box, select a location for the file.

3 From the Format (Mac OS) or Save As Type (Windows) menu, select either PNG or JPEG. Select Use Artboards, then click All or enter a Range value.

4 Click Export. The JPEG or PNG Options dialog box will open.

   ▪ In the JPEG Options dialog box, set the Quality slider to between 5 and 7.

   ▪ In the PNG Options dialog box (**Figure 17.9**), from the Resolution menu, select Screen (72 ppi). From the Background Color menu, select Transparent.

5 Click OK to export the file to the preferred format.

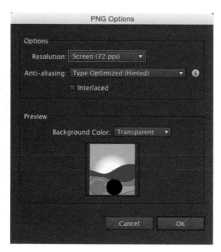

Figure 17.9 The PNG Options dialog box

Export to SVG Format

SVG is a vector format that describes images as shapes, paths, and optimized effects. SVG files are small and display as sharp-edged shapes on the web and on mobile devices. SVG shapes can be scaled onscreen without any loss to their clear, sharp edges.

1 Choose File > Save As. In the Save As dialog box, select a location.

2 From the Format (Mac OS) or Save As Type (Windows) menu, select SVG. Select Use Artboards, then click All or enter a Range value.

3 Click Save. The SVG Options dialog box opens.

4 From the SVG Profiles menu, select SVG 1.1. Leave the Type menu set to SVG.

5 If the Illustrator file contains any linked placed images, select Embed from the Image Location menu. This will make the images part of the SVG file.

6 Click OK to export the file to SVG format.

NOTE *The November 2015 update of Illustrator CC featured improvements in SVG export. The command is now accessed via File > Export > SVG; the SVG Options dialog box has also been simplified; and there is a new option called Minify that will generate simpler, cleaner code. Give it a try.*

Place as a Smart Object in Photoshop

If you need to bring Illustrator artwork into Adobe Photoshop, the best way to preserve the sharp edge quality of the vector art is to place the file as a Smart Object.

Place Method

A Smart Object is a special layer type in Photoshop. Any vector art placed as a Smart Object will preserve its vector outline information and will be converted, on output, to the resolution of the output device, not the resolution of the Photoshop file.

To place Illustrator artwork, in Photoshop:

- Choose File > Place Embedded to embed a copy of the Illustrator file into the Photoshop file.

- Choose File > Place Linked to link the Illustrator file to the Photoshop file.

Resize the artwork bounding box, then press Return or Enter. The artwork will display in the document and a new Smart Object layer will be listed on the Layers panel.

TIP *The contents of an embedded or linked Smart Object in Photoshop can be opened and edited in Illustrator. When you switch back to Photoshop, the Smart Object will update automatically.*

Figure 17.10 The Paste dialog box in Photoshop. Click either Smart Object or Shape Layer to place the artwork as a vector object.

Copy and Paste Method

An alternate way to bring vector art into Photoshop, and preserve the vector paths, is to use the Copy and Paste commands.

1 In Illustrator, select one or more objects. Choose Edit > Copy.

2 Switch to Photoshop, then choose Edit > Paste.

3 In the Paste dialog box (**Figure 17.10**), select Smart Object to create an embedded Smart Object or select Shape Layer to create a vector shape layer.

Creative Cloud Libraries

Illustrator CC gives you access to the Creative Cloud (CC) Libraries panel and its file sharing features.

1 In Illustrator, choose Window > Libraries to display the Libraries panel. If necessary, click Create New Library to name and create a new library.

2 Drag one or more objects into the Libraries panel. The objects will be copied as a graphic asset to the Graphics category on the panel (**Figure 17.11**).

3 Switch to Photoshop CC and choose Window > Libraries to display the Libraries panel in Photoshop.

Figure 17.11 Drag vector artwork into the Libraries panel to create a graphic asset.

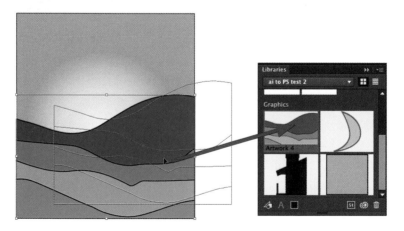

4   Drag the Illustrator graphic into the Photoshop document. Resize and reposition the bounding box, then click Return or Enter (**Figure 17.12**).

A library-linked Smart Object will be created and linked to the CC Libraries asset, not to the Illustrator file.

> **TIP** *To place the Illustrator graphic from the Libraries panel as an embedded Smart Object (with no library link), Control-click (Mac OS) or right-click (Windows) its graphic thumbnail in the panel and select Place Copy from the context menu.*

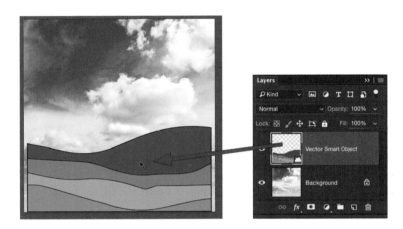

Figure 17.12 In Photoshop, drag the graphic from the Libraries panel into the document.

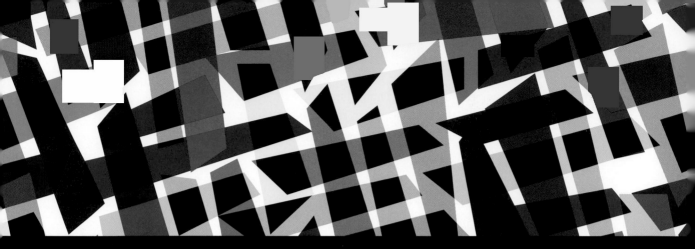

CHAPTER OBJECTIVES

Chapter Learning Objectives

- Learn how to create design work for others and understand their needs and purposes.

- Understand copyright concerns related to the design industry.

- Understand project management concepts and issues related to working as part of a design team.

- Be aware of common problems and pitfalls in project design and in the design industry.

Chapter ACA Objectives

DOMAIN 1.0
SETTING PROJECT REQUIREMENTS

1.1 Identify the purpose, audience, and audience needs for preparing graphics and illustrations.

1.2 Summarize how designers make decisions about the type of content to include in a project, including considerations such as copyright, project fit, permissions, and licensing.

1.3 Demonstrate knowledge of project management tasks and responsibilities.

1.4 Communicate with others (such as peers and clients) about design plans.

DOMAIN 5.0
ARCHIVE, EXPORT, AND PUBLISH GRAPHICS USING ADOBE ILLUSTRATOR CC

5.1 Prepare images for web, print, and video.

5.2 Export digital graphics and illustration to various file formats.

CHAPTER 18

Working with Outsiders

As a designer, you need to work with others. Being a designer and being an artist are two different careers, but most people who do creative work for a living need to do both. If you love to shoot old, crumbly walls and rusty farmhouse doors, you will find that you simply can't pay the bills with your "rusty hinge" photo collection. So a lot of photographers shoot weddings to pay the bills. It may not be their favorite type of photography, but it pays well and makes people happy.

Aside from the money, you will probably learn to develop an immense passion for creating designs for others. The secret to this part of the job is twofold: really listen and really *care*.

NOTE

This chapter supports the project created in Video Project 18. Go to the Video Project 18 page in the book's Web Edition to watch the entire project from beginning to end.

▶ *Video 18.1*
Introduction to Project Planning

Who You're Talking *For* and Who You're Talking *To*

The first step in designing for a particular project is to understand the **client's needs**. This is critical because, among other things, the client pays the bills. Most of all, the client is hiring you to speak for them. For a designer, that's a weighty responsibility. You are being trusted to communicate for an entire company or cause. Therefore, you first and foremost need to address that client's needs and goals for the project. This will be the guiding principle when answering design questions. You must constantly remember your goals and focus narrowly on them to streamline your workflow and minimize distractions.

★ *ACA Objective 1.1*
★ *ACA Objective 1.3*

Let's look at a few example scenarios:

- Rockin' Zombies is a metal-opera-jazz-bluegrass fusion band that wants to promote an upcoming free concert at the local farmer's market.

- Hoi Polloi Church needs a brochure for its project to solicit volunteers and donations to help orphaned children recover from Hurricane Sally.

- OfficeHome Custodial Services wants a flyer to share with businesses about its upscale, environmentally friendly office cleaning services.

- Zak's Bulldozer wants to promote its tree-removal service, which uses low-impact tools, for residential homes.

- The city's health department wants a campaign to promote healthy eating and active lifestyle changes and to inform and warn people about common bad habits.

- Pop-Lite is a new, collapsible photo light, and the inventors need a logo and image for their Kickstarter campaign.

Each project has different goals, right? Some want to give away something. Some want to make money. Some want to solicit help from others. It's important to help the client pin down their project goals—and that can be difficult to do.

★ *ACA Objective 1.1*

▶ *Video 18.2*
Discovering Client Goals

Single Voice, Single Message

Here's a brainteaser. You have 20 close friends, and you can no longer understand what they say. Why? They are close enough to talk to one another. They are all speaking your language. They are all speaking loudly enough for you to hear clearly. They have no health or physical impairments. So what's happening?

They're all talking at once!

If a design says too much, it says nothing. It becomes "noisy" and makes it difficult for the viewer to focus on the main idea. This reality is similar to the design concept of *focal point*. Design projects have a kind of focal point too. It's important to clearly define and pin down the most important goals of a project. Sometimes, clients are trying to clearly define their company purpose, vision, or dreams for their organization. Hearing the overall goals and dreams for the business are *very* helpful in the design process, and necessary so that you understand your client. But to get a project done efficiently—and create a project that communicates well—you must work with the client to establish and narrow the goals for *this particular project* (**Figure 18.1**).

Figure 18.1 Be sure you have a clear and concise understanding of the client's goals for the project.

The short version of a campaign's goals is often called the "elevator pitch" because it summarizes the project in the time that it would take for an elevator ride. It's communicating your purpose in a short, simple sentence. I normally push a client to shoot for seven words or fewer. The goal is to clearly define the goals for this particular design project.

Here are some elevator pitches related to the previous scenarios:

- Come to our free concert.
- Help child victims of a disaster.
- Subscribe to our news service.
- Remove trees without damaging your yard.
- Get healthy and avoid hidden dangers.
- Buy fun and functional little photo lights.

Admittedly, these pitches are not elegant or enticing. There's no "pop" to the message. But they *are* the very core of what you're trying to communicate. It is the reason your client is paying you to design the art. You'll need more detail than this to produce the *best* design, but focusing on this core goal can help you rein in the insidious forces of project creep. But first, let this sink in:

The client's goals are the #1 priority.

If the goal is unclear, the finished product will be unclear. Figure out the goal and you can always come back to it as a "home base" when the project starts to grow or lose its focus. Sometimes the goal isn't obvious or turns out to be different than it first appeared. But it's always critical, and one of your first jobs is to help the client focus on the primary goal of the project. Nonetheless, at the end of the day, you work for the client, so the client calls the shots, has the final say, and makes the decisions—even if you disagree.

Now let's talk about the second most important person on the project—the one who doesn't really exist. I'm talking about the ideal audience.

★ *ACA Objective 1.1*

Ideal Ivan and Danielle Demographic

In real life, you shouldn't judge people, make assumptions, and lump them together. But we do. And as designers, we must. This is called developing a "demographic" for the project and "identifying the target audience." It's a critical step in helping your clients bridge the gap to the audience they want to reach. You do this by identifying the common characteristics of that audience and creating an image in everyone's minds of the typical customer: Ideal Ivan and Danielle Demographic. Some clients will say "everybody needs my product," but those clients will still need to focus on a specific target demographic for *this project*. As the old saying goes, "Aim at nothing, and you'll hit it every time." Those are wise words, especially when identifying a target audience.

▶ *Video 18.3*
Finding the
Target Audience

Identifying a target demographic (**Figure 18.2**) for your project is a critical step, second only to defining the client goals. And generally, it's also a part of those client goals. For example, when you want to create a new fishing pole, you can easily picture your target audience: people who fish. So you're probably not going to use the same graphics, words, images, and *feel* as you would to reach a punk rock audience. And at the same time, expectant mothers probably wouldn't be drawn in by images that would reach your fish or punk target.

Creating a demographic helps you focus on *who* should get your message. It's understanding the goals of your listener/viewer as well as the speaker, your client. You need to make sure you share information in a way that will connect to or resonate with that audience. And if you understand what your audience needs and feels, you can show how what you're offering meets those needs.

The easiest way to do this is to create imaginary "perfect fits" for your client's project. Here are some points to consider:

- **Income:** Determine whether you want to focus on quality, exclusivity, or price.
- **Education:** Establish the vocabulary and complexity of the design.
- **Age:** Dictate the general appeal, attitude, and vocabulary.

- **Hobbies:** Help choose images, attitudes, and terms and phrases unique to their interests.
- **Concerns, cares, and passions:** Identify core beliefs, trigger points, and so on.

Figure 18.2 Once you have identified your target audience, you'll know how to speak their language.

It's pretty easy to see how different audiences will need different images. You don't want images of extreme sports in an ad aimed at expectant mothers. You wouldn't use a crowded nightclub image in a design for a camping and canoe outfitter company. It's a pretty obvious concept, but inexperienced designers sometimes design to please themselves, and that isn't always what pleases the target audience.

What makes your audience unique? Who has the problems that this product solves? Have those pictures in your mind. Work these ideas over with your client and help them envision their typical customer. Then look for images that will appeal to that ideal customer, this project's target demographic.

Think of yourself as a matchmaker. You're trying to introduce your client to the perfect customer or consumer. Speak in the language that the ideal clients would want to hear, and use images that will bring their lifestyle and outlook together with your client.

The Golden Rule for Client Projects

▶ *Video 18.4* *The Golden Rule for Client Work*

Design is about helping others with their vision. It's about communicating a message. So when it comes down to it, use the business version of the golden rule: He who has the gold makes the rules.

Ultimately, you work for your clients. Help them see what you regard as the most effective way to reach the audience and identify the right questions to ask, but don't fight with them. Your clients have insight or perspective about their target audience that you are unaware of. When you disagree with clients about a design decision, help them realize their vision for their project. If you don't like it, you don't have to put the final piece in your portfolio, but you'll still get to put their check in your bank. If it comes down to what the client wants versus what you think the identified audience will respond to, do what the client asks. It's the client's project, audience, and money (**Figure 18.3**).

Figure 18.3 He who has the gold makes the rules. Help your client achieve their goal, even if you don't completely agree with it.

This rule has one exception that you need to follow at all times. When your client asks you to skirt copyright law, you are still responsible to respect the law and your fellow designers. Often your client is just confused, and you can help them understand that you can't copy other designs or use copyrighted materials without authorization. Along those lines, let's take a moment to talk about copyright.

Copyrights and Wrongs

Copyright is actually an amazing set of laws that seeks to protect and promote artists along with their art, creativity, and learning. It's gotten a really bad rap, but you should set aside any preconceived ideas for a bit and think through the copyright concept (**Figure 18.4**).

★ *ACA Objective 1.2*

Figure 18.4 Copyright can be a complex issue, but the basics are straightforward.

Copyright law is misunderstood by many people, so understanding it is an awesome way to score high on trivia night. You may also help your struggling author and artist friends realize that they don't have to pay an attorney tons of money to "make sure they get their stuff copyrighted." You can do it for them, or show them how to do it themselves. It's free and easy. As a matter of fact, it's probably already done.

Keep in mind that I'm a teacher and writer, not a lawyer. This chapter is not legal advice; it's just intended to help you understand the law and the reasons it exists so you can appreciate it. It's easier to obey a law that you understand and appreciate, and copyright laws protect our rights.

Copyright law promotes freedom and creativity. Let's explore how.

Copyright Happens

▶ *Video 18.5* *About Copyright*

The first thing to know is that copyright just happens. If something can be copied, then it's copyrighted. You needn't fill out any special forms, report to a government office, or do anything extra to put it in place. The law is written so that copyright happens as soon as something original and creative is recorded in a "fixed form." This means that as soon as you write something down, sketch it out, code a chunk of elegant programming, or click the shutter on your camera, whatever you just recorded is copyrighted. The only reason you might take any additional steps is to establish verifiable proof of *when* a creation was copyrighted, because the person who can prove that he or she recorded it first owns the copyright.

Imagine that you're in a restaurant talking with a friend. During this conversation you make up a song on the spot. A famous singer in the booth behind yours hears you and writes it down. He claims the copyright to those lyrics and makes a million bucks with your spontaneous song, and there's little you can do about it. However, if you recorded it on your phone when you sang it, you recorded it in fixed form *first*. So, *you* own the copyright to the lyrics, and the artist now owes *you* a truck full of money. Kind of weird, right?

Why does the law have this quirky little rule? Because the courts have to decide who actually owns copyright when its ownership is contested. And courts rely on tangible proof. So the law makes it simple by stating that he or she who first records something in fixed form wins. That way, if you have no proof that you were first, you're not going to try to sue someone. But even if you were first, if you can't prove it you're out of luck.

So why are there copyright notices on music, DVDs, and one of the first pages of this book? If we don't need it, why do we display it?

Simply put, it reminds people who owns the copyrighted material. If the date and copyright symbol were not displayed on this book, people might think they could legally make photocopies of it for their friends. Most people assume that if no copyright notice appears, then no copyright exists. (They're totally wrong.) The presence of a visible copyright statement discourages this conclusion and behavior.

Figure 18.5 You don't need this mark or any sort of label, but it does show others that your work is copyrighted.

So it certainly won't cause any harm to scratch a copyright symbol (©) on your art when you're finished with it (**Figure 18.5**), but it's more to remind *the public* than to protect *you*. You're already protected by law. Adding the copyright symbol to your work is like putting one of those security system signs in your front yard. It won't stop a really determined thief, but it can deter less-committed offenders. If you think it destroys the look of your front yard, you don't need it for protection.

Placing a Copyright Notice in Digital Content

The beauty of digital files is that they have the ability to contain hidden information that never compromises the enjoyment of the document itself. As a result, you can add copyright information to digital content without having a visually distracting copyright notice on the artwork. You do this by adding information known as **metadata** to your digital files.

Metadata is information that doesn't show up on the document itself, but is hidden inside the file. This is a perfect way to store copyright information, contact information, and so on. On some digital cameras, metadata can even record the lens information, the location via GPS, whether a flash was attached and fired, the camera settings, and more. In digital files, metadata can share the computer on which it was created, the time, and even the name of the creator. Be sure to use metadata when you're sending your work out over the web. If you use a web developer to place your designs in a web page, ask them to include your copyright info. You should also check files that your clients give you to make sure that you're not violating another designer's means of making money when you're trying to make some yourself.

"But I'm not trying to make any money with their art, so it's okay, right?" Well, that's a tough question with a few interesting rules attached.

Playing Fair with Copyrighted Material

Can you use copyrighted material when you're learning to use Illustrator? Can you make a funny image using a movie poster by replacing the faces of the actors with the faces of your friends? What about using cool images from your favorite video-game that you include on a web page you're making in a web design class?

All these uses are completely legit. The people who came up with the copyright laws were very careful to make sure that the laws don't limit—but rather promote—creativity. They did this with a set of ideas known as **fair use**.

Fair use policy is a set of rules that make sure copyright protection doesn't come at the cost of creativity and freedom. Copyright can't be used to limit someone's

▶ **Video 18.6** *Digital Tools for Tracking Copyright*

NOTE

Metadata is how good technology teachers catch cheaters.

▶ **Video 18.7** *Fair Use and Copyright*

personal growth or learning, freedom of speech, or artistic expression and creative exploration. Those ideas are more important than copyright, so copyright doesn't apply when it gets in the way of those higher ideals. You are free to use copyrighted materials in the pursuit of those higher goals. Some people (mistakenly) believe that fair use doesn't apply to copyrighted materials; but in fact, it applies *only* to copyrighted materials. Here is a list of issues that a court would consider when making a decision about fair use:

- **Purpose: If you used the work to teach, learn, voice your own opinion, inspire yourself to create a new piece of art, or report news, you're probably safe.** Protected reasons include educational purposes (teaching, research), freedom of speech (commentary or criticism), news reporting, and transformative work (parody or using the work in a new way). It isn't considered fair use if you're making money from the use, using it just for entertainment, or trying to pass it off as your own work.

- **Nature: If the nature of the original work was factual, published information, or the work was critical to favoring education, you're probably safe.** Was the content already published, fact based, and important for society to know? Then you're pretty safe to use the work. But if it was unpublished, creative (such as art, music, film, novels), and fictional, you're probably *not* cleared to use it.

- **Amount: If you use a small amount of a copyrighted work, it's more likely that your use of the work was fair use.** If you used only a small quantity—not the main idea or focus of the work, or just enough to teach or learn from—you're probably safe. If you used a large portion of the work or basically ripped off the central idea or the "heart of the work," it isn't fair use.

  For example, if you see a web design composition that includes a nice rollover button effect that you want to emulate by writing your own code that achieves the same result, you're on solid ground. Taking the entire composition and simply changing a few names and labels and publishing it as your own work would be a violation of copyright.

- **Effect: If nobody was harmed because of the action you took, then your action was probably fair use.** If you used a legitimate copy of the original work, it didn't affect the sale of another copy, and you had no other way to get a copy, you're in pretty good shape. But if your copy made it less likely that someone would buy the original or you made a large number of copies, you're probably hurting the original creator, and that's not fair use.

As mentioned, copyright law really tries to address a simple question: How can we promote more freedom and creativity in the world? This is the question that copyright laws seek to answer. Fair use makes sure that beginning artists can experiment using anything they want. Just be sure not to share anything that might be another artist's copyrighted work.

But as a beginning designer, how can you get quality assets to use in real-world projects? Happily, you have access to more free resources than ever before via the Internet and free stock photo sites. Let's look at some.

Uncopyrighting

You have a couple of ways in which to undo copyright. One is voluntary. An author can choose to release the copyright to their material. Believe it or not, this can be more difficult to do than you'd expect. Copyright law really tries to protect creators, and it can be difficult to *not* be protected by copyright law.

▶ *Video 18.8*
Licensing Strict and Free

The second way is to let the copyright expire. Copyrights normally expire from 50 to 100 years after the death of the original author, but exceptions to this rule and extensions can be requested. It's beyond the scope of this book to discuss copyright at length, but it is important to realize that some materials have expired copyrights. When copyright is expired or released, the work is said to be in the public domain. This means that copyright no longer applies to the content, and you can use the material without worrying about infringement.

Licensing

Licensing is another way that you can legally use copyrighted material. For designers and artists, licensing is fairly common because it allows you to use copyrighted material, for a certain time and in a certain way, by paying a fee established by the copyright holder according to the use of the material.

Stock photos are popular items licensed by Photoshop designers, and you can find them from many sources at varying prices. Stock photos are images for which the author retains copyright, but you can purchase a license to use these images in your designs. For almost everyone, this is a much less expensive solution than hiring a photographer to go to a location and shoot, process, and sell you the rights to an image.

CREATIVE COMMONS

In the last decade or so, a lot of exploration has been done in finding creative ways to license creative works. **Creative Commons** licensing is built upon copyright law, but it offers ways that artists can release their works for limited use and still choose the way the works are used and shared.

Creative Commons licenses include many different combinations of the following attributes and use many different symbols to identify the type of license (**Figure 18.6**), so you'll need to do some research when using Creative Commons–licensed materials and when releasing assets with Creative Commons licensing.

- **Public Domain** licenses, or "CC0" licenses, allow artists to release their works to the public domain. It's a bit difficult to give your materials away to the public domain, but CC0 is generally recognized as a way to do so and is respected in most parts of the world.

- **Attribution** (marked as "BY") requires that you credit the original author when using their work. You can do whatever you want with the work as long as you give that credit.

- **ShareAlike** (marked as "SA") allows you to republish a creative work as your own creation, but you must provide the same license setting as the original author. This allows others to continue to share the work.

- **NoDerivs** (marked as "ND") requires that you not change the material when you incorporate it into your own work. You can use NoDerivs material freely, but you must pass it along without change.

- **NonCommercial** (marked as "NC") means that people can use your work in their own creative works as long as they don't charge for it. You're getting it free, so if you want to use it, then you have to be generous and also give away your work for free.

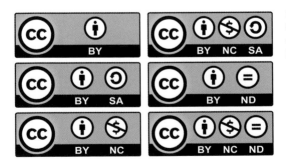

Figure 18.6 Creative Commons licenses allow for a variety of easy-to-understand licensing options.

Creative Commons licenses are widely accepted and used, and you can find a ton of amazing resources that use this licensing. If you have any questions about Creative Commons licenses, you can find out everything, from a general overview to very detailed legal descriptions, at *creativecommons.org*.

PEOPLE PERMISSIONS

If you use pictures of people in a web design project, you'll need a special kind of license known as a **model release**. This type of release is required when a person's face is identifiable in the photo and the image will be used to promote something—whether it's a product or idea. Any work you do for a client is by definition a commercial use and would require a model release for every identifiable face.

Think Like a Boss

Some might say that the only thing you need to know to succeed in life is how to solve a problem (**Figure 18.7**). That's not how to solve a *specific* problem—that would be only an exercise in memory. A well-trained monkey can mimic a person's actions and get a similar result, but he can't think with the depth of a human. My personal preference for solving problems is to work to understand things deeply and explore all the nuances of a potential solution. But for others, this process is a little outside their comfort zone and they find it faster and easier to copy someone else's solution.

Figure 18.7 Make sure you stop to plan before working on your idea—it saves more time than it takes.

In the graphic design world, copying another solution might mean following tutorials or using designs that have been posted on websites where designers display and freely share their work.

But what do you do when you're the leader? What happens when you need to do something new and fresh for your job? What if the boss doesn't know how to do it and that's why they hired you? How do you respond when the client's main request is "Do something that hasn't been done before."

That's where the problem-solving process comes in—the only skill you really need to be successful. If you can do that, you can figure out anything.

★ *ACA Objective 1.3*

▶ *Video 18.9* *Project Management Intro*

Project Management

Project management is really just the problem-solving process in action—geared toward supervising resources, people, and team-based projects. The DNA of project management is problem solving and organizing the process so that you tackle the right issues at the right time using the right tools. Project-management systems take on a million forms (as do problem-solving systems), but if you truly grasp the ideas behind the labels, you can translate them into whatever management strategy your client, team, or boss is using.

The problem-solving process is creative in itself. A good solution to a problem can be artistic in its elegance and efficient grace. A problem solved well can be *beautiful*. This is the most important section of this whole book, because if you can grasp problem solving, you can learn whatever you need to learn now and in the future. Here is where we shove you out of the nest.

The following process will help when you need to solve a technical problem on hardware or equipment, handle a design problem within Illustrator, or figure out how to get your hand out of that jar you got it stuck in. It will help you translate a tutorial written for Illustrator CC into your current version (things change fast these days). And it boils down to three simple steps: **learn, think, and do.**

Learn

▶ *Video 18.10* *Project Management— Understand the Problem*

The first step of a problem-solving process is to learn. It includes two important steps: learning what the problem is, and learning how others have solved similar problems (research and investigate). It seems simple, but the process can be confusing. Most projects with major problems get stuck at this initial step because they didn't learn well—or at all. Let's talk about them.

UNDERSTAND THE PROBLEM

I talked about understanding the problem earlier in the chapter; the first step of every project is to understand the problem. For most design projects, you must figure out how to most effectively help your client share goals with the target audience. If the client is yourself, then it's about getting to the essence of what you want to communicate and to communicate it so that your target audience can act on it.

Mess it up here, and by definition you are not solving the problem. You haven't properly identified it, so how can you solve it? You might be solving *a* problem, but you're not solving *the* problem. Sometimes you can actually make the problem worse by implementing a plan that creates a new problem without solving the real one.

You can avoid trouble down the road by clearly understanding and defining the problem at the start. "I want to sell a million widgets" is not a problem you can solve; it's a desire the client has. So what's the problem you can help with? They haven't sold as many as they want to? That's not it either. How do you get to the bottom of the problem?

Start with good questions (**Figure 18.8**): Do people need a widget? If so, do people know that widgets are a thing? If so, do they choose a competing widget? If so, why do they choose this other widget? Why do you think they should use your widget instead? Who would be most likely to buy your widget? What is your budget for widget advertising? What do you want to spend on this particular project? What are your expectations?

Figure 18.8 Nailing down the client's goals and preferences at the beginning of the project will help you develop an efficient plan.

Many clients become frustrated with this set of questions. They just want to see some action so that they can feel like they're doing *something*. But let me repeat that old saying: "Aim at nothing, and you'll hit it every time." This is when you sharpen your axe so you don't have to bang at the tree all day.

This part of the project can be fairly informal on smaller projects, but it can be huge on large projects. Here's a list of critical questions to answer:

- **Purpose:** Why are you doing this design project? What result would you consider a success?
- **Target audience:** Who needs this message or product? Describe your typical customer.
- **Limits:** What are the limits for the project? Budget and time are most necessary to nail down.
- **Preferences:** Aside from the results already discussed, are there any other results you'd like or expect from this project?
- **Resources:** Does the client already have the artwork, video, or other resources that need to be included? Are they in a format that's ready for the web?

These examples are intended to show how quickly you can determine a client's expectations. The answers to these questions define the size of the job and how you'll best be able to work with the client.

Sketches and written notes from this initial step will help. Gather as much information as you can to make the rest of the project go smoothly. The more you find out now, the less you'll have to redesign later because the client hates the color, the layout, or the general direction you took the project. Invest the time now, or pay it back with interest later. With a clear idea of what the problem is, you'll get the information you need to solve it in the next step.

RESEARCH AND INVESTIGATE

After you understand exactly what your client is expecting, you can start doing the research to arrive at the answers you need. Let's take a quick look at that word: *re-search*. It literally means "search again." Lots of people fail to *re-search*; they just search. They look at the most obvious places and approaches, and if things don't immediately click, they settle for a poor but quick and easy solution.

Depending on the job, research can be a relatively quick process. Find out about the competitive products, learn about the problem you're trying to solve, and understand the demographic you're going to target. Sometimes this can be done in your initial conversations with the client, but for larger projects you may need to spend more time and go as far as creating proofs of concept to help you define possible solutions. The main thing is to be sure to analyze the problem, and look for ways that others have solved similar problems. Again, the more research you do, the better information you'll have about the problem you're trying to solve, which will help you with the next step.

Think

The next couple of steps represent the "thinking" phase. You can do this quickly using a pen and napkin, or you can do it in depth and generate tons of documentation along the way, particularly on large projects. But thinking is the part that most of us often mistake as the beginning. Remember that if the learning step isn't done well, your thinking step might be headed in the wrong direction.

▶ *Video 18.11*
Project Management— Think It Through

As a designer, you'll often do much of your thinking on paper (**Figure 18.9**). Sketch it out first and have that reference to show the customer, and come back to it for clarity.

Figure 18.9 Sketch first and establish clarity.

BRAINSTORM

As with "re-search," you need to really grasp the meaning of brainstorm. It's a brain*storm*. Not a brain *drizzle*. A full-on typhoon of ideas (**Figure 18.10**). It's critical—*absolutely critical*—that you get out of the "analyze" mode of thinking and into your "creative" mode. They are two different mind-sets. Actually, they're opposite mind-sets. If you start thinking critically instead of creatively, you've changed direction and you will lose ground on your brainstorming task. If you start moving in the critical direction, that's the opposite of creative. Stop that! Don't try to work hard on brainstorming. Work relaxed instead.

Figure 18.10 Brainstorming is an inherently disorganized and messy process—clean up your ideas later.

But sometimes analysis happens. You start analyzing how to complete your ideas when you should be creating them. Here are some of the things that trigger the critical mode of thinking. Don't do them when brainstorming.

- **The No-No's:** Judging your ideas. Trying to finish an idea when you should still be brainstorming. Getting stuck on a particular idea. Planning out the project. Thinking about how much time you have. Thinking about the budget. Thinking about numbers. Grouping or sorting your ideas. Developing the idea that you think is best. Choosing a solution because the technology is cool.

Here's what you should be doing:

- **The Go-Go's**: Listen to music. Look at cool art online. Call a friend. Doodle something. Read a poem. Take a break. Go for a walk. Listen to some comedy radio. Write a haiku. Meditate for five minutes. Exercise. Sleep on it.

When you're in brainstorming mode, don't edit your ideas. Let them flow. If a crummy idea pops into your head, put it on paper. If you don't, it will keep popping up until it's been given a little respect. Give the weak ideas respect. They open doors for the great ones. Brainstorming is completely a matter of creating ideas.

PICK AND PLAN

After brainstorming, you need to pick a solution that you generated in your brainstorming session and plan things out. You'll find that the plan you go with is rarely your first idea. Through the process of brainstorming, the idea will go through several iterations. A common mistake for beginners is to fall in love with an early idea—beware of this pitfall (**Figure 18.11**). Your best idea is lurking in the background of your mind, and you have to get rid of all the simple ideas that pop up first. For a small project or a one-person team, you might quickly hammer out a contract and get to work, but in larger projects, the planning needs to be detailed and focused.

▶ *Video 18.12*
Project Management— Get It in Writing

Figure 18.11 Resist the urge to fall in love with early ideas—the best ideas come near the end.

The larger the project, the more formal this process will be. Small projects with just one person working on them will need little planning for moving forward. But larger projects will need a project plan to set the project requirements for the team.

SETTING PROJECT REQUIREMENTS

This is where the action happens. Look through the ideas you've generated, pick the one that seems best, and plan how to make it happen. This is where you determine exactly what needs to be done, establish some direction, and identify a clear target. Did you catch that last sentence? This planning stage (which most creative types naturally tend to resist, myself included) is where you clarify what needs to be done, establish your direction, and identify a clear target. We resist it because it seems to limit us. It ropes in our creative freedom and gives us a checklist—things that many creatives hate. These things are creative kryptonite—or at least we *think* they are. But let's really consider this for a moment.

If you don't perform this admittedly tedious step, what won't you have? You won't have a definition of what needs to be done, a direction to head in, or a target to hit. Everyone will be in the dark. Although this step doesn't seem creative in itself, creativity isn't the priority at this particular juncture. You're at a journey moment versus a destination moment. Creativity without limits is a journey, which is great for your own work but a disaster for a client-driven job. A client-driven project requires clearly defined goals—a destination. You need to arrive somewhere specific (**Figure 18.12**).

Figure 18.12 A well-developed plan with sketches will ensure a smooth working relationship with the client.

Two critical points that need to be a part of every project plan are the project scope and the project deadline. Every contract needs to have these critical components defined to focus the project and make it clear to everyone involved the "what" and "when" of the project.

- **Project scope** is the amount of work to be done. On the designer's side, this is the most important thing to establish. If the scope isn't clear, you're subject to the Achilles heel of design work: project creep. This is a pervasive problem in our industry (and I'll address it later in detail), but simply writing down a defined scope can prevent the problem. Get in writing *exactly* what you need to do, and make sure specific numbers are attached.

- **Project deadlines** dictate when the work needs to be done. This is the client's most important element. The deadline often affects the price. If the client needs ten designs or illustrations in six months, you can probably offer a discount. If they need art by tomorrow morning, then they'll have to pay an additional "rush" fee. Deadlines on large projects also can be broken down into phases, each with its own fee. This division of tasks helps you pay the bills by generating cash flow during a large and lengthy project. It also limits the impact—for you—of payment delay.

These items, when shared and discussed with your client, will save time, money, and disagreements. These additional **deliverables** are the raw materials of project planning and help convey the exact target of the project. It's my opinion, and that of experienced designers, that the following two deliverables are critical for every design project.

- **Sketches** are really helpful to show the client your design direction. Even better is when the client has an idea of what they're looking for and can give you their own sketch. Does this limit your creative freedom? Yes! It also saves you a ton of time. The goal of a client job is to get a project done to their satisfaction. If they are very particular and know what they want, you're not going to convince them otherwise. Sketches save time because they limit your direction to a direction that the client will accept, and they help you get to that acceptance faster. That means you finish and get paid sooner. The better the sketches are before you get into actual design, the fewer changes and redesigns you'll need. You don't need to be a master sketch artist. Just convey the idea. Sometimes sketches may just be **wireframes**, very rough representative sketches of how to lay out the document.

- **Specifications** are detailed, clear written goals and limits for a project. Many times, the specifications themselves will be referred to as the "project plan" and become part of the contract. This is admittedly the least creative and most boring document you will create, but it is also the most critical. All project plans should include two critical pieces of information: the scope of the project and the deadlines that need to be met. Be sure to *always* include *both* of these items in your project specifications.

AVOIDING PROJECT CREEP

▶ *Video 18.13*
Project
Management—
Avoiding Creep

No, the **project creep** is not the person on your project who stares at you from around the corner. That *is* creepy, but that's not the meaning. Project creep is when the project starts to lose its focus and spin out of control, eating up more and more time and effort (**Figure 18.13**). It is really important to be aware of this phenomenon. It happens all the time. And the main culprit in every case is a poorly designed project plan that lacked clear specifications and deadlines.

Figure 18.13 A project can appear small but have lots of issues under the surface. A solid contract will avoid this becoming your problem.

Here's how it happens: Joe Client creates a product and wants to sell it. He comes to you for marketing materials. You determine that he wants a logo, a flyer, and a three-page informational website. A price of $2500 is settled on, and you've got a month to get it done. You go to work.

Then Joe realizes that he also wants some images for social media. Could you just make a few? He also realizes that he needs to put his new logo on new business cards. Could you just design a card with the logo on it? Oh, and he can't figure out how to get his product onto his favorite online marketplace. Could you just help him set that up? And he changed his launch date. He doesn't need it next month; he needs it next week because he just reserved a booth at a large convention. By the way, do you know anything about designing booths? Can you see how critical it is that you create a detailed project plan with task definitions and deadlines attached? Sometimes the client asks for something and it takes you 30 seconds. It's a good idea to always happily deliver on these little items. A favor is any job that takes you five minutes or less. After that, the favor turns into work. And your only defense is a contract defining a clearly stated scope.

Just make sure that the project's scope is clearly stated. If the contract says that you'll provide *any* images for the company's identity presence, then you're in trouble. On the other hand, if it specifically says that you'll provide up to nine images for a print brochure and a website, then you're in great shape. Taking the hour it requires to specify your project and its deadlines in detail will save you from many hours of work and contract revisions.

If the client approved a sketch with a basic layout and then asks for something different, you need to charge them for the change—if it's going to take more than 5 to 10 minutes. Sticking to this policy helps the client think about changes before sending them to you. If you fail to charge when addressing impromptu changes, the client has no reason to think about the requests in advance. Charging your customer for additional changes focuses them on what they really want.

Of course, if the client asks for something that actually makes the job easier and faster, then make the change and do it for free. The bottom line is this: Establish good will whenever it's good for both you and your client. But when an eleventh-hour alteration serves only one side of the relationship, the requesting side has to pay for the service. In the end, this arrangement ensures that everyone ends up winning and that the client regards you as the professional that you have become.

Do

▶ *Video 18.14*
Project
Management—
Make It So

The last phase of the project plan is to knock it out. This is the "two snaps and a twist" phase because it generally happens pretty quickly when you have a good plan—unless there's a hitch. (I'll get to that soon.) But at this point, on most design projects, you're pretty much wrapping things up.

BUILD IT

This step is pretty obvious: Make it happen. This phase is where most people think all the action is. But honestly, if you've done the prior steps well, this can be the fastest part of the process. You already know what to do; now just do it. The design decisions have been made and you get to work. Of course, when doing this step, it's best to regularly refer to the specifications and keep the client informed. The best way to do so is to have a very intentional feedback loop in place.

FEEDBACK LOOP

★ *ACA Objective 1.4*

A **feedback loop** is a system you set up to constantly encourage and require input and approvals on the project direction. Keeping your client informed is the best way to speed through the process (**Figure 18.14**). For an Illustrator project, **iterative work** establishes effective guideposts to send to the client for review and input. Iterative work is work you're sharing as it's done. Doing so performs a couple of critical functions. First, it lets the client see that work is being done and reassures them that the process has momentum. Second, it lets the client chime in on anything that they don't like while it's still easy to make a change.

Figure 18.14 A good feedback loop helps ensure that what you are thinking is what the client will approve.

Establishing this open communication channel encourages and enforces a healthy exchange of opinions and can enable you to most efficiently adjust and fine-tune your project to suit your client.

TEST AND EVALUATE

This very last step can also be fast if you've had a good feedback loop in place. For Illustrator projects, it's essentially checking the work against your project plan and making sure that you met all the specifications to satisfy you and your client (**Figure 18.15**). If not, you should essentially start the problem-solving process again to understand the current problem. Find out exactly what, according to the client, doesn't meet the requirements.

Figure 18.15 If the project meets all the specifications in your project plan, you're done!

Assuming a good project plan with sketches and a good feedback loop, the evaluation phase should require just minor tweaks—no different than any other iterative work resolution. If you didn't have a good feedback loop and the first time the client sees your work is upon delivery, that client could become really unhappy and demand innumerable changes. Avoid this migraine headache with an effective and well-defined feedback loop as part of your well-developed plan. Those two tools are your weapon against project creep and unreasonable clients.

WORKING FOR "THE MAN"

Many graphic designers and illustrators begin their careers working at larger firms, where they use Ilustrator to create designs for clients. This can actually be a much easier way to get started than freelancing with your own business. If you're exclusively a designer, this type of job may require you to do the only tasks you're best

▶ **Video 18.15** *The Advantages of Working at a Firm*

at doing. In a large firm, someone else does the sales, manages client relationships and projects, and creates technical specifications. As a designer in a larger firm, you would be responsible for working on some or all of the design. Everything else is done by someone else, which is a good trade-off if you are more into being visually creative and less into handling the many aspects of project management.

Working within an experienced company can also be an amazing education, as you can develop your strengths, learn about the industry, and slowly increase your involvement in the other aspects of this career beyond Illustrator proficiency.

Conclusion

★ ACA Objective 1.1

★ ACA Objective 1.3

▶ **Video 18.16**
*Wrapping Up
Project Planning*

Much of this chapter digressed from the hands-on Illustrator stuff that most books cover. But the lack of this information can present a problem for many beginning artists and designers. You need to master a lot of industry information, creative knowledge, and business skills to be successful. Many creative people have a hard time with the business side of the career, but it's best to understand these ideas and concepts now before a lack of understanding becomes a problem. The tips and techniques that you've read in this chapter will truly help eliminate a lot of the inherent frustration in the complexity of working with and for other people. Illustrator is a creative application and tends to attract creative types. The qualities that make us great at thinking outside the box and designing new and beautiful images are the same qualities that may make us less skilled at the organized detail work of business and client management.

ACA Objectives Covered

DOMAIN OBJECTIVES	CHAPTER	VIDEO
DOMAIN 1.0 Setting Project Requirements		
1.1 Identify the purpose, audience, and audience needs for preparing graphics and illustrations.	**Ch 18** Who You're Talking *For* and Who You're Talking *To*, 199 **Ch 18** Single Voice, Single Message, 200 **Ch 18** Ideal Ivan and Danielle Demographic, 202	**18.1** Introduction to Project Planning **18.2** Discovering Client Goals **18.3** Finding the Target Audience
1.2 Summarize how designers make decisions about the type of content to include in a project, including considerations such as copyright, project fit, permissions, and licensing.	**Ch 18** Copyrights and Wrongs, 205	**18.5** About Copyright **18.6** Digital Tools for Tracking Copyright **18.7** Fair Use and Copyright **18.8** Licensing Strict and Free
1.3 Demonstrate knowledge of project management tasks and responsibilities.	**Ch 18** Project Management, 212 **Ch 18** Who You're Talking *For* and Who You're Talking *To*, 199	**18.9** Project Management Intro **18.10** Project Management—Understand the Problem **18.16** Wrapping Up Project Planning
1.4 Communicate with others (such as peers and clients) about design plans.	**Ch 18** Feedback Loop, 222	**18.12** Project Management—Get It in Writing **18.13** Project Management—Avoiding Creep **18.14** Project Management—Make It So **18.15** The Advantages of Working at a Firm

continues on next page

continued from previous page

DOMAIN OBJECTIVES	CHAPTER	VIDEO
DOMAIN 2.0 Understanding Digital Graphics and Illustrations		
2.1 Understand key terminology related to digital graphics and illustrations.	Glossary, 230	
2.2 Demonstrate knowledge of basic design principles and best practices employed in the digital graphics and illustration industry.	**Ch 19** Leveling Up with Design, 19-3 **Ch 19** Creativity is a Skill, 19-4 **Ch 19** The Design Hierarchy, 19-5 **Ch 19** The Elements of Art, 19-9	**19.3** Design School: The Design Hierarchy **19.4** Design School: The Elements of Art **19.5** Design School: The Element of Space **19.6** Design School: The Element of Line **19.7** Design School: The Element of Shape **19.8** Design School: The Element of Form **19.9** Design School: The Elements of Texture and Pattern **19.13** Design School: The Principles of Design **19.14** Design School: The Principle of Emphasis **19.15** Design School: The Principle of Contrast **19.16** Design School: The Principle of Unity **19.17** Design School: The Principle of Variety **19.18** Design School: The Principle of Balance **19.19** Design School: The Principle of Proportion or Scale **19.20** Design School: The Principles of Repetition and Pattern **19.21** Design School: The Principles of Movement and Rhythm **19.22** Design School: Wrapping Up Design School
2.3 Demonstrate knowledge of typography and its use in digital graphics and illustrations.	**Ch 19** The Element of Type, 19-29	**19.12** Design School: The Element of Type
2.4 Demonstrate knowledge of color and its use in digital graphics and illustration.	**Ch 19** The Element of Color, 19-24	**19.10** Design School: The Element of Value **19.11** Design School: The Element of Color

DOMAIN OBJECTIVES	CHAPTER	VIDEO
2.5 Demonstrate knowledge of image resolution, image size, and image file format for web, video, and print.	**Ch 17** Resolution for Rasterized Effects, 189	
DOMAIN 3.0 Understanding Adobe Illustrator CC		
3.1 Identify elements of the Illustrator CC user interface and demonstrate knowledge of their functions.	**Ch 1** Using the Main Interface Elements, 4	**Intro 01** Work Area
3.2 Define the functions of commonly used tools, including selection tools, the Pen tool, and other drawing tools, shape tools, and transformation tools.	**Ch 3** Reshape a Corner, 31 **Ch 5** A Primer on Paths and Selection, 47 **Ch 6** Align Two Circles with Precision, 63 **Ch 13** Draw with the Pen Tool, 135	**Project 01-01** Basic Shape—Live Shapes **Project 01-03** Basic Shape—Live Corners **Project 03-01** The Pen Tool
3.3 Navigate, organize, and customize the workspace.	**Ch 1** Workspaces, 11 **Ch 2** Navigating the Illustrator Interface, 21	**Intro 03** Workspaces
3.4 Use non-printing design tools in the interface, such as rulers, guides, bleeds, and artboards.	**Ch 2** Artboards, 17 **Ch 6** Precise Alignment of Objects, 61	**Project 01-08** Yin Yang Logo
3.5 Demonstrate knowledge of layers and masks.	**Ch 5** Layers Panel (First Look), 57 **Ch 16** Create a Clipping Mask, 176	**Project 05-03** Creating a Clipping Mask
3.6 Manage colors, swatches, and gradients.	**Ch 4** Working with Fill and Stroke, 37 **Ch 10** Add Gradient Fills, 101	**Project 01-02** Basic Shape—Fill and Stroke **Project 01-04** Basic Shape—Shapes for Robot **Project 02-03** Knife Tool and Gradients
3.7 Manage brushes, symbols, graphic styles, and patterns.	**Ch 12** Open Symbol Libraries, 122 **Ch 14** The Brushes Panel, 147	**Project 02-06** Work with Symbols **Project 03-05** Apply a Brush

continues on next page

continued from previous page

DOMAIN OBJECTIVES	CHAPTER	VIDEO
3.8 Demonstrate knowledge of how and why illustrators employ different views and modes throughout the course of a project, including vector/outline vs. display/ appearance, isolation mode, and various Draw modes.	**Ch 8** Isolate a Group, 87 **Ch 16** Clip Via Draw Inside Mode, 177	
3.9 Demonstrate an understanding of vector drawing tools.	**Ch 13** Draw with the Pen Tool, 135 **Ch 14** Create an Object with the Blob Brush, 156	

DOMAIN 4.0 Creating Digital Graphics and Illustrations Using Adobe Illustrator CC

4.1 Create a new project.	**Ch 2** Create a Document, 15	**Intro 02** Create a New Document
4.2 Use vector drawing and shape tools.	**Ch 3** Basic Geometric Shapes, 27 **Ch 5** Reshape an Oval to Make a Straight Hair Strand, 49 **Ch 6** Use the Shape Builder Tool, 65 **Ch 7** Apply Effects to an Object, 77 **Ch 12** Symbolism Tool Specifics, 129 **Ch 14,** Paint a Brush Stroke, 149	**Project 01-05** Draw Faces via Reshape **Project 03-06** Watercolor Effect **Project 03-07** Create/Edit Brushes **Project 03-08** Custom Brushes **Project 03-09** Sketch with Paintbrush
4.3 Transform graphics and illustrations.	**Ch 3** Remove a Point, 35 **Ch 5** Transform Objects to Create Variation, 50 **Ch 7** Reshape via Transformation, 71 **Ch 8** Distortion Tools, 82 **Ch 9** Create a Live Paint Group, 91 **Ch 11** Blend Two Objects, 112 **Ch 13** Convert Points, 139 **Ch 16** Expand a Tracing, 179	**Project 01-06** Introduction to Live Paint **Project 01-07** Live Paint Part 2 **Project 02-01** Gears **Project 02-02** Creating Spirals **Project 02-04** Blending Basics **Project 02-05** Work with Blend Steps **Project 03-02** Trace an Image with the Pen Tool **Project 03-03** Freehand Drawing with the Pencil Tool **Project 03-04** Trace a Photo with the Pencil Tool **Project 05-05** Applying a Logo to a Perspective Drawing—Part 1 **Project 05-06** Applying a Logo to a Perspective Drawing—Part 2

DOMAIN OBJECTIVES	CHAPTER	VIDEO
4.4 Create and manage layers.	**Ch 5** Layers Panel (First Look), 57 **Ch 6** Stack an Object Behind, 68 **Ch 8** Group Objects, 86	**Project 04-01** Creating Point Type **Project 04-02** Working with Text Flow and Text Wrap **Project 04-03** Placing Type on a Path or Inside an Area **Project 04-04** Using 3D Effects and Creating Type Outlines **Project 04-05** Letter Shapes into Logos **Project 04-06** Using Type and Shapes in a Logo **Project 04-07** Placing Type on a Circular Path **Project 04-08** Creating a Story Layout Using Type and Graphics
4.5 Import assets into a project.	**Ch 16** Place Bitmap Images as Embedded Objects, 173 **Ch 16** Use Image Trace, 178	**Project 05-01** Placing Embedded Images **Project 05-02** Using Image Trace **Project 05-04** Embedded Images vs. Linked Images
4.6 Add and manipulate type using Type tools.	**Ch 15** Type, 159	**Project 04-01** Creating Point Type
4.7 Create digital graphics and illustrations using 3D and perspective tools in Illustrator.	**Ch 16** 3D Mapping, 181 **Ch 16** Use Perspective Grid Feature, 181	**Project 05-07** Logos on Perspective Grid **Project 05-08** Constructing an Interior Using Perspective—Part 1, 183 **Project 05-09** Constructing an Interior Using Perspective—Part 2, 183 **Project 05-10** Constructing an Interior Using Perspective—Part 3
DOMAIN 5.0 Archive, Export, and Publish Graphics Using Adobe Illustrator CC		
5.1 Prepare images for web, print, and video.	**Ch 17** Prepare Artwork for Print Output, 186	**Project 05-11** Output
5.2 Export digital graphics and illustrations to various file formats.	**Ch 2** Save a Document, 20 **Ch 17** Export Artwork, 193	**Intro 04** Save a Document

Glossary

additive color Created by combining light. Color components are red, green, and blue. When added together at 100%, the three components create white.

Adobe Bridge An Adobe application that enables you to view thumbnails of your files and helps you sort and organize those files. It gives you centralized access to all your Illustrator files and to other media assets you may need for your projects. In Illustrator, the Go To Bridge button is located on the Application bar.

alignment Indicates how the lines are aligned on the right and left edges, such as left, centered, and right.

all caps Uses only uppercase letterforms for each letter.

analogous (colors) Colors that are side by side on the color wheel. They create gentle and relaxing color schemes.

anchor point A point connecting two segments on a path. An anchor point can be either a corner point or a curved point. See also *corner point, curved point*, and *smooth anchor point*.

appearance The attributes that are applied to an object and that are listed on the Appearance panel.

Application bar The bar at the top of the Application frame. The bar contains the Go To Bridge button, the Arrange Documents menu, the workspace switcher menu, and the Search for Help field. In Windows, the main Illustrator menus also appear on this bar.

Application frame The frame that surrounds the Illustrator interface and contains the Application bar, document windows, and panels, and select zoom and artboard navigation options.

area type A type object (consisting of many lines of text) where type wraps to fit within a vector shape.

Arrange Documents menu Located on the Application bar, this menu contains options for viewing multiple document windows in various horizontal or vertical arrangements within the Application frame.

asymmetrical Achieves balance using elements with different weights or values on each side (or the top and bottom) of an image.

attributes The settings such as fill, stroke, effects, and opacity that are applied to an object. The attributes of an object make up the object's appearance.

attribution Written acknowledgment provided with the name of the original copyright holder of the work. Creative Commons and other licenses feature different kinds of attribution requirements.

balance Evenly distributed, but not necessarily centered or mirrored.

blackletter fonts Also known as Old English, Gothic, or Textura. Feature an overly ornate style. Convey a feeling of rich and sophisticated gravitas.

bleed The part of the image extending past the cut edge to ensure an edge-to-edge print.

blend A multistep color and shape progression between two separate objects. Blends are created via the Blend tool or the Make Blend command.

cast shadow The shadow cast on the ground and on any objects that are in the shadow of the form. Shadows fade as they get farther from the form casting the shadow.

chaotic lines Look like scribbles and feel unpredictable and frantic. Convey a sense of urgency, fear, or explosive energy.

clipping mask A special group of objects in which the topmost object crops (masks) the objects that are below it. Portions of the lower objects that extend beyond the path of the topmost object are hidden and don't print. The topmost object in a clipping mask is referred to as a clipping path.

color The perceived hue, lightness, and saturation of an object or light.

color harmonies Color rules that are named for their relative locations on the color wheel.

complementary (colors) Colors that are opposite each other on the color wheel. They are high in contrast and vibrant.

compound object An object contained within one or more smaller, transparent paths that creates a hole in the larger object. The hole can be removed by releasing the compound object and separating the paths into individual objects.

compound shape An object created via the Shape Modes options on the Pathfinder panel. The individual objects that are combined into a compound shape are preserved and can be edited or released at any time.

context menu A temporary menu of options that display in various Adobe programs when you right-click the mouse on a particular object or portion of a panel. Options in a context menu change based on the type of object or where in the interface you click.

contrast Creates visual interest and a focal point in a composition. It is what draws the eye to the focal point.

Control panel The panel in Illustrator that contains controls, links (to temporary panels), and settings. Options on the panel change depending on the type of object currently selected.

convert a point Change an anchor point from corner to curved or vice versa. You can convert points via the Anchor Point tool or via options on the Control panel.

corner point An anchor point that connects either two straight line segments or a straight and a curved segment on a path.

Creative Cloud Libraries A feature provided in Illustrator that enables you to copy artwork as an asset into a Libraries panel, then place that asset into any other Adobe application that also contains a Libraries panel. Library assets are stored in your Creative Cloud Assets page.

Creative Commons Ways that artists can release their works for limited use and still choose the way the works are used and shared: Public Domain, Attribution, ShareAlike, NoDerivs, and NonCommercial.

curved (line) Expresses fluidity, beauty, and grace.

curved point An anchor point that connects two curved segments on a path. When selected, direction handles will display to control the shape of the curved segments.

decorative fonts Also known as ornamental, novelty, or display fonts. They don't fall into any of the other categories of fonts. Convey a specific feeling.

deliverables A predetermined list of items that will be delivered to the customer.

design elements The building blocks of art defined by artists to provide a framework for creating art.

design principles The essential rules or assembly instructions for art.

diagonal (lines) Lines traveling neither on a vertical nor a horizontal path. Express growth or decline and imply movement or change.

dingbat fonts Also known as wingdings. They are a collection of objects and shapes instead of letters.

direction A common way to describe lines, such as vertical, horizontal, or diagonal.

direction handle A visual feature that displays on a selected curved anchor point that controls the shape of a curved segment.

dock The vertically stacked arrangements of panels on the right side of the Application frame. You can customize the arrangement of panels in the dock and create additional docks.

document color mode Determines the color model that Illustrator uses to create the image, such as RGB or CYMK.

document window A tabbed window within the Application Frame that contains the artboards and canvas scratch area.

dpi Stands for dots per inch and refers to the resolution of an image when printed.

drawing modes Illustrator provides three specific drawing modes: Draw Normal (the default), Draw Behind, and Draw Inside. Draw Behind places newly drawn objects behind selected objects. Draw Inside places newly drawn objects within a selected object.

elements of art The building blocks of creative works. They are the "nouns" of design, such as space, line, shape, form, texture, value, color, and type.

embedded Placing a bitmap image as a non-vector object in an Illustrator document. The image data is stored in the document. See also *linked*.

emphasis Describes the focal point to which the eye is naturally and initially drawn in a design.

face In Illustrator, the area formed by intersecting lines in a Live Paint group.

fair use A set of rules that specify how and when copyrighted material can be used and that make sure copyright protection doesn't come at the cost of creativity and freedom.

feedback loop A system set up to continually encourage and require input and approval on a project's direction.

fill Solid color, pattern, or gradient that is applied to the interior of a vector object. The current fill color displays in the Fill square on several panels in Illustrator.

flow A category related to the energy conveyed by lines and shapes.

focal point What the design is all about. The call to action or the primary message you are trying to get across.

fonts The whole collection of a typeface in each of its sizes and styles.

form Describes three-dimensional objects, such as spheres, cubes, and pyramids.

geometric (lines) Tend to be straight and have sharp angles. Look manmade and intentional. Communicate strength, power, and precision.

geometric shapes Predictable and consistent shapes, such as circles, squares, triangles, and stars. They are rarely found in nature and convey mechanical and manufactured impressions.

glyph Each character of a font, whether it is a letter, number, symbol, or swash.

gradient fill A gradual blend between two or more solid colors. Gradients are created and edited via the Gradient panel in Illustrator.

group A collection of objects on an artboard that can be selected as an entire unit for editing and organizing elements in a design. On the Layers panel, a <Group> listing will display and the collection of objects will display as individual listings nested within the group.

hand-drawn (line or shape) Appears as though created using traditional techniques, such as paints, charcoal, or chalk.

handwritten fonts Also known as hand fonts, they simulate handwriting.

highlight The area of a form that is directly facing the light and that appears lightest.

horizontal Moving from left to right; for example, the horizontal line in an "H." Expresses calmness and balance.

hyphenation Determines if and when words should be split with hyphens when wrapping to the next line.

ideographs (ideograms) Images that represent an idea, such as a heart representing love.

implied lines Lines that don't really exist but are implied by shapes, such as dotted or dashed lines, people waiting in lines, or the margins of a block of text.

indent Settings that determine how far an entire paragraph is indented from the rest of the text on each side or in just its first line.

isolation mode A special viewing and editing mode that is activated by double-clicking an object or a group. All other objects are temporarily dimming, thereby limiting editing to only the selected objects.

iterations New versions of a design that successively become closer to the desired result.

iterative work Work that is shared as it is completed, allowing the customer to chime in with comments while it is still easy to make a change.

join To unite two endpoints into one point on a path. Points can be joined via the Join tool.

justified Aligns text to a straight edge on both the right and left edges of a paragraph.

kerning The space between specific letter pairs.

layers A way to organize objects and put some objects in front of, or behind, others. When objects are on separate layers you can temporarily lock or hide them to facilitate editing objects on other layers in the same area of the artboard.

leading The amount of space between the baselines of two lines of text in wraparound paragraph type. Increase the leading value to increase the amount of white space between lines of text.

licensing A way to legally use copyrighted material for a certain time and in a certain way, usually associated with paying a fee established by the copyright holder.

ligatures Special characters used to represent letter combinations, such as "fi."

light source The perceived location of the lighting in relation to the form.

lightness A color setting affecting tone, from darker to lighter.

line A mark with a beginning and an end point.

linked Placing a bitmap image as a screen version of an image in an Illustrator document. A link is established between the placed image and the original source image. Image data is not stored in the document. See also *embedded*.

Live Corners A feature for non-rectangular objects such as polygons that displays a corner widget for controlling the corner radius on a selected corner point.

Live Shapes A feature for rectangle or rounded rectangle objects only that displays corner widgets for controlling the corner radius on a selected object. See also *shape properties*.

metadata Information that is included in a document but is hidden, such as copyright, lens information, location via GPS, camera settings, and more.

model releases The permission that is required when a person's face is identifiable in a photo and the image will be used to promote something—whether it's a product or an idea.

monochromatic Different shades and tints of the same color. Communicates a relaxed and peaceful feeling.

monospaced fonts Fixed-width or non-proportional fonts that use the same amount of horizontal space for each letter.

movement Visual movement within an image, such as the natural tracking of the eye across an image as the eye moves from focal point to focal point.

negative space Blank areas in a design. Also known as white space.

NoDerivs Creative Commons licensing. Requires that you not change material when you incorporate it into your own work. It can be used freely, but you must pass it along without change.

NonCommercial Creative Commons licensing. Means you can use work in your own creative work as long as you don't charge for it.

object Any created vector shape or placed image in an Illustrator document. An individual object can be selected for editing and is listed on the Layers panel as a <Path>.

object shadow The area of the form that is facing away from the light source and appears darkest.

organic Describes lines, shapes, or forms that are irregular and imperfect, as those found in nature.

organic lines Lines that are usually irregular and imperfect. Found in nature.

organic shapes Are random or generated by something natural. They are usually asymmetric and convey natural, homemade, or relaxed feelings.

panel group A tabbed grouping of multiple panels, usually located in a dock.

panels The highly customizable interface elements containing common tools, settings, and options that can be easily moved, rearranged, or resized.

paragraph settings Affect an entire paragraph rather than selected words. These settings include alignment, space before/after, hyphenation, and so on.

paragraph spacing Similar to leading, but applies to the spacing above or below the entire paragraph (and not to the lines within the paragraph).

paragraph type A type object (consisting of many lines of text) where the type wraps to fit within a text rectangle.

path The edge of a vector shape or line. A path technically has no dimension, so a stroke must be added to make it visible.

path type A type object where type follows along the edge of an object's path.

pattern A repetitive sequence of different colors or shape objects. You can use the Pattern Options panel to create custom patterns that can be applied as a fill or stroke on a path.

pictograph (pictogram) Graphic symbol that represents something in the real world. Computer icons are pictographs that suggest the function they represent, such as a trash can icon to delete a file.

pixel A single dot that makes up a raster image. Pixel is short for "picture element."

point type A type object (consisting of just one character or several words of text) that stands by itself and is not associated with any drawn path or object. Point type can be positioned anywhere on an artboard.

points Used to measure type size, approximately 1/72 of an inch.

ppi Stands for pixels per inch and is a setting that affects only printed images. Higher ppi affords more detail in printed images. While vector objects are resolution-independent, raster effects, and rasterized objects and images need to have a ppi value applied to produce quality output.

Preferences dialog box A dialog box that contains various options and settings that are applied to all Illustrator documents you create. The dialog box organizes the options and settings into specific categories and displays each category in a custom panel. Preference settings can be changed at any time.

primary colors Colors that cannot be created by combining other colors, and can be combined to create every other color in the visible spectrum. Additive color systems such as a computer use the primary colors of red, blue, and green (not red, blue, and yellow as in painting).

printer's marks Marks printed along the outer margins of a printed sheet (beyond the page boundary). These marks are indicators to help printers determine such items as trimming the paper, aligning color separation films, and evaluating the color quality of each the separate inks used to print color.

process colors Colors that are defined as a combination of the four CMYK (Cyan, Magenta, Yellow, and Black) ink colors. Process colors are used when printing artwork to devices that create color using these four inks.

project creep Unplanned changes that increase the amount of work, or scope, that a project requires. When the project loses focus and spins out of control, eating up more and more time and effort.

project deadlines Dictates when work needs to be completed.

project scope Outlines the amount and type of work to be completed.

proportionately An option that can be set when scaling an object to preserve the current width-to-height ratio of an object.

public domain Creative Commons licensing. When copyright is expired or released and no longer applies to the content or when an artist releases their work. It can be used without worrying about infringement.

radial Circular type of balance that radiates from the center instead of the middle of a design.

raster Originally described an image created by scan lines on CRT monitors, but today it is basically synonymous with bitmap. Certain effects in Illustrator are referred to as "raster" because they are composed of pixels and not vector shapes.

rasterize To convert a vector object into a raster/bitmap image.

reflected highlight Area of a form that is lit by reflections from the ground or other objects in a scene.

repetition Repeating an element in a design.

representative shapes Shapes used to represent information. They are helpful in communicating with multicultural and multilingual audiences.

resolution A measurement of the number of pixels in a given space—either in an inch (ppi) or pixel dimensions (such as 1920x1080).

rhythm Creative and expressive, rather than a consistent pattern or repetition in a design.

rule of thirds A technique for laying out the space of your page to provide a focal point. Two vertical and two horizontal lines evenly divide the space into nine equal boxes, as in a tic-tac-toe board.

sans serif fonts Text without serifs. Often used for headlines and titles for their strong, stable, modern feel.

saturation The level of pure color versus white or gray in a color less white or gray means a more vivid, or saturated, color.

script fonts Mimic calligraphy. They convey a feeling of beauty, grace, or feminine dignity.

secondary colors Created when you combine primary colors.

serif fonts Fonts with serifs the little "feet" on character ends, created by typewriters. They convey tradition, intelligence, and class.

shape A reference to an area enclosed by an outline, such as geometric shapes or hand-drawn shapes. In Illustrator, shapes are also referred to as objects when talking about the actual elements in the artwork.

shape properties The middle portion of the Transform panel that displays shape and corner settings for a selected object drawn with the Rectangle or Rounded Rectangle tool. See also *Live Shapes*.

ShareAlike Creative Commons licensing. Allows you to use an item (design) in any way you want as long as your creation is shared under the same license as the original work.

sketches Representative drawings of how to lay out a document or web page. These are sometimes one of the deliverables of a project.

slab serif fonts Squared-off versions of a typical serif font. Also known as Egyptian, block serif, or square serif. Convey a machine-built feel.

small caps Uses only uppercase letterforms for each letter and appears in a smaller size.

smooth anchor point A curved anchor point. See *anchor point*.

Smooth curve Two segments that create a continuous, symmetrical curve on either side of an associated anchor point. Direction handles for a smooth curve always move in tandem to preserve the smoothness of the curve.

space The canvas, or working area. Its dimensions are determined by the resolution of the page you are creating.

specifications Detailed written goals and limits for a project. These are sometimes one of the deliverables of a project.

stock photos Images for which the author retains copyright but for which a license for use is available.

stroke Solid color, pattern, or gradient applied to the edge of a vector object. To make the stroke visible, a weight (width) and color need to be applied to the object. The current stroke color displays in the Stroke square on several panels in Illustrator.

stroke weight The thickness (width) applied to a stroke on the edge of a path.

style (line) An effect applied to a line, such as varying width, hand-drawn, and implied.

subtractive color The familiar model of mixing red, yellow, and blue ink or paint to make colors. We see the colors because of subtracted light.

swashes Special characters with flowing and elegant endings for the ascenders and descenders.

symbol A predefined, reusable design element accessed via the Symbols panel.

symbolism tools A set of eight tools used to edit symbols contained within a symbol set.

symmetrical Occurs when you can divide an image along its middle, and the left side of the image is a mirror image of the right (or the top reflects the bottom). Conveys an intentional, formal, and mechanical feeling.

tertiary colors Created by mixing primary and secondary colors.

texture Describes the actual tactile texture in real objects or the appearance of texture in a two-dimensional image.

Tools panel Contains all the tools that you can use in Illustrator. It's important to know that most icons on the toolbar provide access to a group of hidden tools when you click and hold on the tool's icon.

trace Convert shapes in a bitmap image into vector paths. In Illustrator, this can be done manually via the Pen tool or automatically via the Image Trace panel.

tracking The overall space between all the letters in a block of text. It allows you to compress or expand the space between the letters as a whole rather than just between specific pairs, as you do with kerning.

type size A font's height from the highest ascender to the lowest descender.

typeface Specific letterform set, such as Helvetica, Arial, Garamond, and so on. It is the "look" of letters.

unity Also known as harmony and sharing similar traits. Low contrast. Things that go together should look like they belong together. The opposite of variety.

value Lightness or darkness of an object. Together with color, represents the visible spectrum, such as a gradient.

variety High contrast. The opposite of unity.

variable width profile Preset and user-defined settings displayed on the Variable Width Profile menu and applied to an object's stroke.

variable width stroke A stroke that does not have a uniform width. In Illustrator, use the Variable Width Profile menu (on the Control panel) or the Width tool to create a variable width stroke.

varying-width (line) Expresses flow and grace.

vector object An element composed of points connected by straight and curved segments defined by mathematical instructions. Vector object are resolution independent. This means they can be scaled with no loss of edge quality.

vertical scale Describes the function of stretching letters and distorting the typeface geometry.

weight (stroke) The thickness, or width, of a line.

wireframe A schematic sketch of a project, commonly used for interactive projects.

Workspace switcher menu The menu, located on the Application bar, that enables you to choose predefine workspaces and save user-defined, customized workspaces.

workspaces Specific arrangements of the panels within the interface for easy access to features you use often. Illustrator provides predefined workspaces or you can create a custom workspace that suits your workflow needs.

Index